an eye for art

an eye for art

**Focusing on Great Artists
and Their Work**

Presented by the
National Gallery of Art

CHICAGO
REVIEW
PRESS

Produced by the Publishing Office, National Gallery of Art, Washington

Judy Metro, *editor in chief*
Chris Vogel, *deputy publisher and production manager*

Designed by Wendy Schleicher and Rio DeNaro. Edited by Nancy Eickel with assistance by Lisa Wainwright. Production assistance by Mariah Shay.

Typeset in Berkeley Oldstyle and Fago. Printed on Gardamatt by Gruppo Editoriale Zanardi, Padova, Italy.

Display images (all details)

front cover (*clockwise from top*): Jacob Lawrence, p. 92; Vincent van Gogh, p. 60; André Derain, p. 43; Johannes Vermeer, p. 128

frontispiece: Mary Cassatt, pp. 108–109

p. vi: George Bellows, p. 47

back cover (*clockwise from top left*): Winslow Homer, p. 113; Chuck Close, p. 65; Wayne Thiebaud, p. 117; John Constable, p. 4

10 9 8 7 6 5 4 3 2 1

First edition published by Chicago Review Press, Incorporated
814 North Franklin Street
Chicago, Illinois 60610

Library of Congress Cataloging-in-Publication Data

National Gallery of Art (U.S.)

[Essays. Selections]

An eye for art : focusing on great artists and their work. — First edition.

    pages   cm

ISBN 978-1-61374-897-8 (pbk.)

1. Art appreciation—Juvenile literature.
2. National Gallery of Art

(U.S.) I. Title.

N7477.N38 2013

708.153—dc23   2013009403

A catalogue record for this book is available from the Library of Congress and the British Library.

contents

preface

For the past eleven years the National Gallery of Art has issued a family quarterly that included an "Inside Scoop" featuring artists and works from the museum. This book is a collection of those "Scoops"—updated, revised, and expanded. The book is grouped around seven general themes and highlights works from different time periods to encourage comparisons among them. We hope the book will inspire children to explore and develop "an eye for art."

We are grateful to the MSST Foundation for its generosity in making this publication possible and especially to Nancy Furlotti for her personal enthusiasm for the Gallery's mission to engage family audiences.

Lynn Pearson Russell
Head, Division of Education

studying nature

Slowing down to look closely at nature is an art. By examining the colors and shapes of birds or flowers, observing the effects of light at different moments, or noticing the ways a landscape can change over time, artists find inspiration in the natural world. This chapter introduces artists who are captivated by nature and study it closely. John Constable depicted his native English countryside with fresh attention to atmosphere. Martin Johnson Heade and John James Audubon traveled widely to document birds in their natural habitats. Claude Monet cultivated his private gardens as subjects to contemplate, painting them in changing seasons. Georgia O'Keeffe found beautiful abstractions in the details of a single flower. Andy Goldsworthy uses natural materials to create sculptures that often become part of nature. As you study the different artists in this chapter, think about how artists help us see the natural world in new ways.

1 Constable's Country

John Constable (1776–1837) was born in East Bergholt, a village nestled in the Stour River valley of Suffolk County in southeast England. He spent most of his career painting scenes of his native countryside. Dotted with cottages, farms, and mills, the rustic landscape along the river captured his imagination.

His father, a prosperous mill owner and coal merchant, encouraged him to join the family business, but Constable was interested in painting. After seven years, he was finally able to persuade his father to allow him to pursue a career in art. At the age of twenty-two Constable went to London and enrolled in the school of the Royal Academy, the leading British art institution. There he studied the landscapes of past masters—Titian, Peter Paul Rubens, Jacob van Ruisdael, and Claude Lorrain—but he soon decided that he should paint directly from nature.

Returning home to Suffolk each summer, Constable made drawings in the meadows he had known since childhood. Through the close observation of nature, he developed a fresh approach to landscape painting by capturing the effects of light, shadow, and atmosphere.

2 Wivenhoe Park

Major General Francis Rebow, a family friend, asked Constable to paint his country estate, Wivenhoe Park. Constable placed the house in the far center of the composition and featured the estate's park and pasture in the foreground. Look for a flock of birds flying above the elm trees, swans and ducks gliding across the pond, fishermen casting their net from a boat, and cows grazing or resting along the shady bank. On the far left, General Rebow's young daughter drives a donkey cart!

Painting mostly outside, Constable captured the radiance of a summer day with naturalistic details. Covering half the canvas with a bright sky, Constable carefully considered how the billowing clouds interact with the landscape: he painted the pattern of shadows cast by the clouds upon the estate, the play of light over the landscape, and the reflections of sky and trees in the water.

above: John Constable, *Self-Portrait* (detail), c. 1799 – 1804, pencil and black chalk heightened with white and red chalk, © National Portrait Gallery, London

right: John Constable, *Wivenhoe Park, Essex*, 1816, oil on canvas, National Gallery of Art, Widener Collection

3 The Six-Footers

Working in his London studio from 1818 to 1825, Constable completed a series of scenes of everyday working life along the Stour River. He painted from his memories and earlier drawings, and he called the paintings "six-footers" because each canvas was approximately six by four feet in size.

The White Horse, his first six-footer, shows a barge transporting a horse across the river. Using poles, the men work hard to push the barge to the opposite bank where the horse's path continues. These grand paintings of rustic country scenes attracted positive attention at annual exhibitions and helped Constable achieve recognition as an artist.

Painting on such a large scale proved challenging, so Constable developed a unique approach to creating the six-footers. He first made full-scale sketches in oil on canvas that allowed him to try out his ideas and experiment with painting techniques. Since a six-footer took months to complete, Constable used his sketches as a way to plan the composition and determine how to arrange buildings, people, and animals in the landscape.

Compare the sketch of *The White Horse* to the finished painting. Where are the similarities? What are some differences? Constable often painted sketches with looser, more spontaneous brushstrokes and thicker paint, while his finished paintings have a smoother surface and include more details. Look for places where Constable made changes by adding, removing, or rearranging things.

"I do not consider myself at work [unless] I am before a six-foot canvas." John Constable

4 Legacy

Unlike many of his contemporaries (including the British artist J. M. W. Turner), Constable never traveled outside of England. Throughout his life he remained inspired by the landscapes and places he knew and loved, recording both his direct observations of nature and his personal responses to it. Constable's paintings, however, did leave England. Some of his six-footers were exhibited in Paris, where their expressive brushwork and atmospheric effects influenced French artists Théodore Gericault and Eugène Delacroix and later, the young impressionists.

explore more

Cloud Studies

Constable believed artists should combine direct observation, personal experience, scientific understanding, and imagination to create landscape paintings. Fascinated by weather, he studied the new field of meteorology. He became aware of how cloud cover, the ever-changing sky, and atmospheric effects could influence the appearance of nature.

To retreat from the city, Constable took a house in Hampstead, where he could enjoy extensive views across the open countryside. There, in 1821 and 1822, he painted about a hundred oil sketches of clouds and skies. He recorded the sky during different conditions and carefully observed various cloud formations and their movements. Constable called these exercises "skying." On the reverse of the sketches, he often noted the date, time of day, and direction of the wind. These cloud studies later helped him to integrate dramatic skies into his large paintings.

"The sky is the source of light in nature — and governs everything."
John Constable

Keep a cloud journal of your own

With an adult, go outside and find a comfortable place to sit and view the sky. Take a pad of paper and colored pencils or crayons.

Look up and watch the clouds for a while.

Describe the clouds, using these words to get started.

What shapes are the clouds? How much of the sky is covered with clouds? Do they look high or low? List all the colors you see in the sky, from shades of blue and gray to yellow, pink, red, orange, purple, and white.

Record your observations with pictures and words

Make a drawing of the clouds in the sky. Write the date, time of day, and a brief report about the weather.

What would it be like to fly through the sky? Imagine what the earth looks like from up in the clouds.

Repeat this activity every day for a week, once a week or once a month for a year, or whenever you want to enjoy nature or discover a new cloud.

John Constable, *Cloud Study: Stormy Sunset*, 1821 – 1822, oil on paper on canvas, National Gallery of Art, Gift of Louise Mellon in honor of Mr. and Mrs. Paul Mellon

1 An American Naturalist

American painter Martin Johnson Heade (1819–1904) specialized in landscapes, seascapes, and still lifes during his long career. Born the son of a farmer in rural Bucks County, Pennsylvania, Heade began to paint in his late teens after he received art training from a neighbor. At age twenty-four, Heade launched a career as a portrait painter and spent the next fifteen years traveling around the United States and Europe in search of commissions. He was nearly forty years old when he began to paint the New England coastline and salt marshes, subjects whose light and atmosphere would preoccupy him for several years.

Heade began painting hummingbirds in 1862. He had long been fascinated by the tiny birds' quivering movements and jewel-like plumage. The next year, in 1863, he journeyed to Brazil on the first of three expeditions he made to South and Central America. At that time many artists and scientists undertook similar trips to study, draw, and document the exotic plants and animals of the lush tropical rain forests. Heade was particularly interested in the many types of hummingbirds in Brazil, as only the ruby-throated species was found in the northeastern United States. In Brazil, he began a series of small pictures called "The Gems of Brazil," which depicts the great variety of hummingbirds in landscape settings.

In the 1870s, after his final visit to the tropics, Heade lived in New York City. There, relying on his memory as well as on the nature studies he made during his travels, he began to paint another series of hummingbirds with orchids in their natural habitat. This group of works poetically combines Heade's interests in botany, birds, and landscape. *Cattleya Orchid and Three Hummingbirds* is a dazzling example of his inventive compositions.

**"From early boyhood I have been almost a monomaniac on hummingbirds."
Martin Johnson Heade**

2 A Close-up View of Nature

Heade's painting offers an intimate glimpse into a corner of nature. Precisely rendered, the flowers and birds seem to come alive.

Look closely to find:

Three hummingbirds, a Sappho Comet (green with a yellow throat and brilliant red tail feathers) and two Brazilian Amethysts (green with pink throats)

A hummingbird nest

The Cattleya orchid, a bright pinkish-purple flower that is much sought after by orchid collectors and is found in the wild only in Brazil

Moss hanging from tree branches

The mist of the jungle atmosphere

Imagine you have traveled to this place

What sounds might you hear?

What might you smell?

Describe something that would feel smooth or rough.

How would you dress for this trip?

When a rainstorm comes, where might the birds go?

Martin Johnson Heade (detail), 1860, Courtesy of the Miscellaneous Photograph Collection, Archives of American Art, Smithsonian Institution

Martin Johnson Heade, *Cattleya Orchid and Three Hummingbirds*, 1871, oil on wood, National Gallery of Art, Gift of The Morris and Gwendolyn Cafritz Foundation

3 Hummmm...Hummmm...

Hummingbirds got their name because their wings vibrate so rapidly that they make a humming sound. Their wings can beat at a rate of up to two hundred times per second, and the birds can fly through the air at speeds of up to sixty miles per hour. Also, they are the only bird that can fly backward. The smallest of all birds, hummingbirds can weigh as little as two grams. (That's as light as a penny!) Since they have no sense of smell, hummingbirds find their food by sight. There are approximately 340 different kinds of hummingbirds, and they are often called "gems" or "jewels" because of their iridescent feathers.

Heade painted hummingbirds from life, unlike some artists who preferred to use stuffed birds for models. Imagine how difficult it was to study such glittering, flittering creatures!

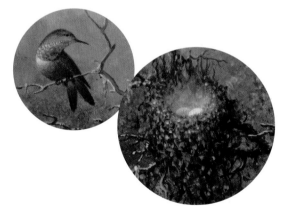

"In the midst of the foliage [the hummingbird] appeared like a piece of lapis lazuli surrounded by emeralds....Everywhere throughout Brazil this little winged gem...abounds."
James C. Fletcher, *Brazil and the Brazilians*, 1857

Audubon's Birds

The French American ornithologist, naturalist, and painter John James Audubon (1785–1851) gave himself a challenge: to record all species of birds in North America. Using the observation skills of an artist and a scientist, Audubon traveled widely and made detailed watercolor, pastel, and graphite drawings of nearly five hundred types of birds. He vividly depicted each bird in its natural habitat, often showing it in motion—hunting, preening, fighting, or flying—and he portrayed each bird life-size. To make the flamingo, swan, and other large birds fit on the page, he presented them in bent positions. Audubon's lifetime of work culminated in *The Birds of America* (1827–1839), an important book that documents all types of birds with 435 hand-colored engravings.

Birding Journal

Look out a window, wander around your yard, or take a walk in your neighborhood or local park. Find a place to sit and quietly observe the world around you. Use a pad of paper or notebook, colored pencils, and a camera to record your observations with words and pictures.

Study the birds you see and take field notes. Describe the colors and shapes of their feet, beaks, and feathers. **Observe** their behaviors. How do they fly, eat, and interact with one another and their surroundings? **Note** the sounds they make. **Imagine** how the world looks from a bird's perspective. **Write** the date and time of day on your field notes. **Make** a drawing of the birds or take a photograph.

Reflect: What did you learn from this experience? Did you see something that you've never noticed before? What else would you like to know?

Repeat this activity every day for a week, once a week or once a month for a year, or whenever you want to explore nature and learn about birds.

Images: Robert Havell after John James Audubon, hand-colored etching and aquatint on Whatman paper, Birds of America, National Gallery of Art, Gift of Mrs. Walter B. James

top left: *Snowy Owl*, 1831, no. 121

top right: *American Flamingo*, 1838, no. 431

right: *Pileated Woodpecker*, 1831, no. 111

"I know I am not a scholar, but meantime I am aware that no man living knows better than I do the habits of our birds.... With the assistance of my old journals and memorandum-books which were written on the spot, I can at least put down plain truths which might be useful and perhaps interesting." John James Audubon

1 Painter and Gardener

French artist Claude Monet (1840–1926) combined his love of nature and art by creating gardens wherever he lived. Although he spent much of his time in Paris and traveled extensively in France and abroad, Monet preferred the countryside and lived for more than fifty years along the Seine River. His interest in gardening grew over the years, from flowerbeds that brightened his first home at Argenteuil to his magnificent gardens at Giverny, which became a pleasure for the eye, a soothing place to contemplate nature, and a source of inspiration.

Monet was especially fond of drawing and painting his own gardens. Over and over again, he showed the ways light, weather, season, and time of day visually changed them. By directly observing nature, Monet captured the momentary effects of light and atmosphere on canvas.

2 At Giverny

In 1883 Monet and his family moved to a former cider farm in Giverny, a small town about thirty-five miles northwest of Paris. He lived there for the rest of his life. At his new home, Monet created a spectacular garden that became the main source of inspiration for his later paintings. The garden was also a living work of art in its own right.

At Giverny, Monet converted part of the farmhouse into a studio, and he transformed the vegetable garden and the neglected two acres surrounding it into complex flowerbeds. He carefully planned out his garden to be beautiful and different as the seasons changed, planting a wide range of annuals, perennials, bulbs, and vines so there were blooms from early spring through late fall. With a painter's eye, Monet thoughtfully arranged plants according to color and height. He liked the flowerbeds to be dense and abundant, overflowing with plants, and he built arbors, trellises, and arches to carry the blossoming color up to the sky.

An enthusiastic and skilled gardener, Monet read horticultural publications, traded seeds, and collected books on gardening. Eventually, the grounds at Giverny became too much for Monet to manage alone, and he hired a team of gardeners. Strict about upkeep, Monet wrote detailed instructions as to when and where to plant seeds and how to prune the shrubs, and he inspected the garden daily.

"My garden is slow work, pursued by love, and I do not deny that I am proud of it." Claude Monet

above: Claude Monet by his waterlily pond at Giverny (detail), summer 1905 (photo: Jacques-Ernest Bulloz), gelatin silver print, Réunion Musées Nationaux / Art Resource, NY

right: Claude Monet in his garden, Giverny (Eure), c. 1915 – 1920 © Pierre Choumoff / Roger-Viollet

In 1903 Monet added a trellis over the bridge and draped it with purple and white wisteria.

"My heart is always at Giverny." Claude Monet

Claude Monet, *The Japanese Footbridge*, 1899, oil on canvas, National Gallery of Art, Gift of Victoria Nebeker Coberly, in memory of her son John W. Mudd, and Walter H. and Leonore Annenberg

4 The Japanese Footbridge

The water garden at Giverny was inspired in part by the distant country of Japan. Monet greatly admired Japanese paintings and prints, especially the landscapes of Katsushika Hokusai and Utagawa Hiroshige that he saw in shops in Paris. He amassed a collection of more than two hundred prints and decorated the walls of his home at Giverny with them. Monet planted Japanese peonies and bamboo around the curving banks of the waterlily pond to evoke the feeling of a Japanese garden. He built an arched, wooden footbridge based on the bridges he studied in Japanese prints.

Painted in the summertime, *The Japanese Footbridge* is one of a series of views Monet made in 1899. The pond nearly fills the canvas, and the sky is indicated only through its reflection on the water. Pink, yellow, and white lilies float on the shimmering surface of the pond, and the foliage and grasses along the banks are mirrored in the water. Spanning the width of the painting, the bridge arcs over the water with its curved reflection below.

Utagawa Hiroshige (1797–1858), *The Drum Bridge from the Wisteria Arbor on the Precincts of the Tenjin Shrine at Kameido*, 1856, from One Hundred Famous Views of Edo, Allen Memorial Art Museum, Oberlin College, Ohio, Mary A. Ainsworth Bequest, 1950

A master artist of woodblock prints, Hiroshige depicted the contemporary life and landscape of Japan, including famous sites such as the Tenjin Shrine.

3 A Water Garden

In 1892 Monet bought a piece of land across the road from his house for an ambitious project—to create a water garden. Diverting a small stream, he formed a pool and surrounded it with an artful arrangement of flowers, reeds, willow trees, and bushes. The surface of the pond was covered with waterlilies.

Monet was fascinated by water and the way reflections constantly change on its surface. He insisted that his gardeners keep the pond very clean—he even made them dust its surface—so reflections of clouds and sky, trees and shrubs, would appear clearly on the water. The water garden became the focus of Monet's art for the last twenty-five years of his career. He created more than 250 paintings of the waterlily pond.

"I have always loved sky and water, leaves and flowers....I found them in abundance in my little pond." Claude Monet

Rouen Cathedral

The lily pond at Giverny wasn't the only place that Claude Monet painted repeatedly. He created several groups of paintings in which he explored the color, light, and form of a single subject at various times of day: haystacks, poplar trees, views in Venice and London, and the cathedral at Rouen in France.

In the winter of 1892 and 1893, Monet rented rooms across from Rouen Cathedral to paint the view of its looming Gothic façade at different times of day. He then reworked the canvases from memory in his studio at Giverny through 1894, making more than thirty paintings in all.

Monet was impressed with the way light creates a distinct mood at different times of day and year and as weather conditions change. In the Rouen Cathedral series, Monet studied how sunlight transformed the façade of the church, with the ever-changing light playing off the stone architecture.

Look at these two paintings

How do they compare in terms of subject matter, mood, feeling, color, shape, texture, and point of view? List five to ten things that the paintings have in common. Then, list as many differences between the works.

Draw a series

Create your own series of views based on the same subject. Choose a favorite outdoor place, such as a view of your home, school, or neighborhood, that you can observe at different times of the year. Draw the scene using paints, pastels, or colored pencils. Carefully observe the colors and shadows, and try to capture a particular moment in time. Repeat this activity several times at different times of day or season. Examine how light changes the scene, and experiment with different ways of capturing these effects with color.

Reflect: What choices might you make as an artist to express the way a place looks and feels at a particular moment in time?

top left: Claude Monet, *Rouen Cathedral, West Façade, Sunlight*, 1894, oil on canvas, National Gallery of Art, Chester Dale Collection

top right: Claude Monet, *Rouen Cathedral, West Façade*, 1894, oil on canvas, National Gallery of Art, Chester Dale Collection

bottom: West façade of Rouen Cathedral, Clarence Ward Archive, Department of Image Collections, National Gallery of Art Library

"Everything changes, even stone."
Claude Monet

Jack-in-Pulpit – No. 2 *Jack-in-the-Pulpit No. 3*

1 Inspiration from Nature

American artist Georgia O'Keeffe (1887–1986) is known for her paintings of flowers, bones, shells, stones, leaves, trees, mountains, and other natural forms. She first painted flowers when she was a child growing up in rural Wisconsin. O'Keeffe decided to become an artist at the age of twelve, and during her long career—she lived to be ninety-nine years old!—she made more than two hundred paintings of flowers. Some of her favorite subjects were lilacs, daisies, irises, petunias, calla lilies, orchids, sunflowers, roses, and jack-in-the-pulpits.

O'Keeffe's high school art teacher first introduced her to jack-in-the-pulpits during a lesson. Her teacher pointed out the plant's unique shapes and color variations. The artist recalled, "This was the first time I remember examining a flower. . . . She started me looking at things—looking very carefully at details. It was certainly the first time my attention was called to the outline and color of any growing thing with the idea of drawing or painting it."

In 1930 O'Keeffe found jack-in-the-pulpits in the woods near her summer home at Lake George in Upstate New York, and she was inspired to create a series of six paintings. These works show the artist's deep interest in the design of nature.

2 A Unique Flower

The jack-in-the-pulpit is a North American wildflower found in shady, cool woods and swamps. It can grow from one to three feet tall. The plant's shape begins as a sort of green vase (called a spathe) made from a single leaf. A stalk, or spadix, grows in the middle of it. A leaf-hood folds gracefully over the top to protect the tiny flower within the spathe from the wind and rain. Typically green with deep purple or red-brown stripes, the flower blooms from April through June. During late summer and early autumn, the stalk grows a cluster of red berries.

It was named jack-in-the-pulpit because in early New England preachers delivered sermons from covered pulpits in churches. A preacher standing in a pulpit resembles the way a spadix sits inside a hooded spathe.

"When you take a flower in your hand and really look at it, it's your world for the moment. I want to give that world to someone else."
Georgia O'Keeffe

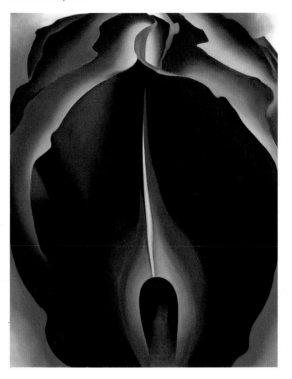

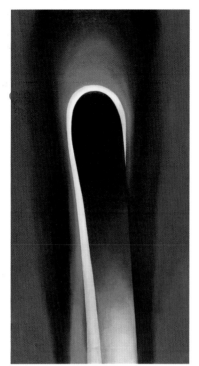

Nos. 2–6: Georgia O'Keeffe, 1930, oil on canvas, National Gallery of Art, Alfred Stieglitz Collection, Bequest of Georgia O'Keeffe

"It is only by deduction, by elimination, by emphasis, that we get at the real meaning of things." **Georgia O'Keeffe**

3 A Closer Look

Concentrating on a single flower, O'Keeffe contemplates the intricate structure of the jack-in the-pulpit. Some of her paintings show curling leaves and sky, and in others the flower fills the entire canvas. Each painting in the series goes deeper inside the center of the flower; with the last one only the jack/spadix is seen. O'Keeffe focuses attention on the flower by magnifying and simplifying its form.

Compare the five paintings. Look for similar elements, such as colors, lines, and shapes.

What do some of the paintings have in common?

What differences do you observe?

Which painting do you find most intriguing? Why?

Alfred Stieglitz, *Georgia O'Keeffe*, 1925, gelatin silver print, National Gallery of Art, Alfred Stieglitz Collection

Photographer Alfred Stieglitz exhibited O'Keeffe's work in New York City. They were married from 1924 until his death in 1946.

"Each shell was a beautiful world in itself.... I have always enjoyed painting them — and even now, living in the desert, the sea comes back to me when I hold one to my ear." Georgia O'Keeffe

Nature Study

One of O'Keeffe's favorite activities was to pick up seashells as she walked along the beach. She displayed her collection at her home in New Mexico, and she often drew her favorite shells. By surrounding herself with objects from nature, she could carefully observe shapes, patterns, colors, and other essential details.

O'Keeffe believed that "to see takes time like to have a friend takes time." It takes a lot of careful looking to get to know something well.

Make a series of drawings

You will need:
A pad of paper
A pencil, colored pencils, crayons, colored chalk, pastels, markers, and/or watercolors

First, select something from nature to study — a flower, leaf, shell, or stone. Place it on a table and sit nearby with your paper and drawing materials. Examine the object carefully. Study its colors, shapes, patterns, and designs. What makes the object unique?

Explore this object in a series of drawings on separate sheets of paper. Try to fill the entire sheet of paper each time as you draw.

Experiment with color

• Use only a pencil to draw the object.

• Draw it again with colors that are as close to the natural object as possible.

• Next, draw it using only two colors.

• Now, draw the object with as many colors as you like. Use your imagination!

Explore design

• Draw the entire object.

• Then, draw a different view. Turn the object around to show another side.

• Select just one detail and draw it as if you were looking through a magnifying glass. Enlarge it to the edges of your page.

• Imagine how the object would look to an insect. Make a drawing showing a "bug's-eye" view of your object.

• Draw the object in an imaginary landscape. Include sky, water, land, animals, and/or buildings in your picture.

top: Georgia O'Keeffe, *The Shell*, 1934, charcoal on laid paper, Lynes 1999, no. 827, National Gallery of Art, From the Collection of Dorothy Braude Edinburg

bottom: Georgia O'Keeffe, *Shell No. I*, 1928, oil on canvas, National Gallery of Art, Alfred Stieglitz Collection, Bequest of Georgia O'Keeffe

1 Stone

British artist Andy Goldsworthy (born 1956) has spent nearly three decades exploring the raw materials of nature, shaping them into poetic and mysterious forms that encourage us to look at our surroundings in new ways. In January 2003, the National Gallery invited Goldsworthy to create a site-specific installation. Completed two years later, in February 2005, *Roof* runs the length of the garden area on the north side of the East Building.

For the installation at the National Gallery, Goldsworthy decided to work with one of his favorite materials: stone. He began by exploring local geology because he is interested in the history of the environments in which he works. Goldsworthy visited quarries in Virginia that once provided stone for many of the historic buildings in Washington, DC. He selected slate, a hard and sharp stone that is often used for roofing.

Goldsworthy, his assistant, and a team of five British dry-stone wallers—experts in the craft of building walls—installed *Roof* during a three-month period, working eight hours a day, six days a week.

previous page: Detail of *Roof* (photo: Lee Ewing © 2004 Board of Trustees, National Gallery of Art)

above: *Collecting boulders near Barre, VT,* 2003, picturing Andy Goldsworthy (photo: Jacob Ehrenberg)

right: *Roof* at the National Gallery of Art's East Building (photo: Lee Ewing © 2004 Board of Trustees, National Gallery of Art)

2 How It All Stacks Up

Roof consists of nine hollow, low-profile domes of stacked slate. Each dome rises five-and-a-half feet off the ground, and together the domes weigh 550 tons.

Goldsworthy used the dry-stone construction method, which does not need mortar to bind the stones together. Weight, balance, and symmetry create the domes' shape and prevent them from collapsing. To accomplish this, the stones are carefully stacked flat; they diminish in size and are cantilevered inward toward the top. Goldsworthy and his team used hand tools and power machinery to size and shape each stone, and they inserted small stone fragments as filler.

Each dome begins with a circular base that is twenty-seven feet in diameter and ends on top with a single, final stone. A circular hole, two feet in diameter, was carved in the capstone, creating an opening called an oculus in each dome.

"There is life in a stone. Any stone that sits in a field or lies on a beach takes on the memory of that place. You can feel that stones have witnessed so many things." Andy Goldsworthy

left: Giovanni Paolo Panini, *Interior of the Pantheon, Rome,* c. 1734, oil on canvas, National Gallery of Art, Samuel H. Kress Collection

right: Aerial view of the National Gallery of Art with the Capitol dome in the background, 1991 (photo: © Dennis Brack / Black Star, National Gallery of Art, Gallery Archives)

3 Domes

Domes are architectural forms that function as roofs and ceilings. A feat of engineering, a dome is a curved structure with no angles and no corners. The earliest domes, Neolithic burial chambers and dwellings, were often made of stone.

One of the best-known domes covers the Pantheon in Rome. Built of bricks and concrete in the second century, this classical structure inspired the design of the domed rotunda crowning the National Gallery's West Building. Each dome has an oculus that lets light into the building.

Since domes are generally roofs, we usually gaze up at them from either the inside or outside of a building. With *Roof,* Goldsworthy brings the dome to the ground. When you study the sculpture from different perspectives, the oculi look like dark black holes.

Goldsworthy has worked with the domical form since the late 1970s, creating domes out of ice, snow, branches, and leaves. With *Roof,* he salutes the long history of the dome and presents an interesting contrast with the East Building's angular, modern architecture. The sculpture even "breaks" through the glass wall that separates the garden and the museum's interior.

Does *Roof*'s cluster of forms remind you of things other than domes?

"Looking into a deep hole unnerves me and I am aware of all the potent energies within the earth. The black is that energy made visible."
Andy Goldsworthy

Andy Goldsworthy, *Working Drawing for Roof,* 2004, Courtesy of the artist and Galerie Lelong

explore **more**

Nature Walk

Goldsworthy works only with materials he finds in nature. Some of the things he uses to create art are:

feathers

stone

ice

moss

sand

flower petals

leaves

twigs

pine cones

wood

thorns

water

snow

Roof is one of Goldsworthy's monumental public works, but some of his sculptures are never seen! Why?

He often likes to work in isolation in nature, where he can experiment with different materials and develop his ideas alone. Many of his works are ephemeral, which means they last only a short time—snow melts, leaves blow away in the wind, sand sculptures on the beach are erased by the rising tide. Goldsworthy photographs his sculptures because they last only a few days, hours, or minutes. The artist welcomes the changes that time brings.

Get closer to nature

Take a walk outdoors! You don't have to go far to discover something new. Don't forget to take an adult companion with you.

Tips for a nature walk

See what natural materials you find as you wander along the way.

Look at the colors and shapes of nature. Study patterns and designs.

Touch different materials. Compare their texture, weight, and size.

Imagine the landscape at another time of day, during another season, or during a rainstorm. What parts of the landscape might change over time?

What did you learn during your walk?

Did you see something that you've never noticed before?

Like Goldsworthy, you might be inspired to make a work of art during your walk. Take a photo to remember it.

Andy Goldsworthy, *Touching north, North Pole*, April 24, 1989 (photo: Julian Calder), image courtesy of University of California, San Diego

"I take the opportunities that each day offers. . . . I stop at a place or pick up a material because I feel that there is something to be discovered. Here is where I can learn." Andy Goldsworthy

How might nature
inspire your own art?

chapter two

exploring places

Artists are often inspired by places where they live or travel, from rural landscapes to bustling cities. This chapter looks at artists who painted familiar places close to home and others who were drawn to lands faraway. Rembrandt van Rijn often sketched the landscape of his native Holland. Canaletto became famous for the paintings he made of Venice, which he sold as souvenirs to visiting tourists. Jasper Francis Cropsey celebrated the Hudson River Valley, particularly its colorful autumn, while both Thomas Moran and George Catlin explored the American West. Henri Matisse and André Derain spent time in the south of France, experimenting with ways to capture the spectacular light of that region. George Bellows was captivated by the energy of a growing New York City. As you explore the artists in this chapter, think about how they describe the unique features of landscapes and cityscapes.

1 Living in a Golden Age

Rembrandt Harmensz van Rijn (1606–1669) was born near the town of Leiden in Holland, where his father owned a mill on the banks of the Old Rhine. The family derived its name from the mill, which was called *De Rijn* (Dutch for "the Rhine"). Years later, after his art career was established, Rembrandt signed his work with only his distinctive first name.

From his youth Rembrandt trained to be an artist. Around 1632 he moved from Leiden to Amsterdam, where citizens of all incomes—from humble crafts-men to wealthy businessmen—bought art objects. In the seventeenth century, Holland was a powerful nation made rich by trading. Amsterdam was the busiest port city in Europe, and its markets sold fab-rics, spices, flowers, fish, and cheese. This period in the nation's history, when art, philosophy, literature, and the sciences flourished, is often called the Dutch Golden Age.

Rembrandt quickly became one of the leading artists in the city. He painted a wide variety of subjects: portraits of middle-class merchants and wealthy professionals, scenes of historic events, and stories from the Bible and Roman mythology. His busy workshop was both a studio and a school where pupils lived, studied, and worked alongside him.

2 Country Walks

Rembrandt didn't always work inside his studio. Often he went for walks in the countryside to observe nature. He took along his sketchbook and made drawings of the rural environment—the farms, marshes, trees, boats, bridges, mills, cottages, and vast sky—that made up Holland's unique landscape.

The Amstel is an important river that had been chan-neled into a canal running right through Amsterdam. Rembrandt followed the river south, out of the city, and sketched *View over the Amstel* looking back toward Amsterdam. Small boats navigate the many canals that crisscross the countryside, transporting goods and people.

above: Rembrandt van Rijn, *Self-Portrait Leaning on a Stone Sill* (detail), 1639, etching, White / Boon 1969, no. 21, State ii / ii, National Gallery of Art, Rosenwald Collection

left: Rembrandt van Rijn, *View over the Amstel from the Rampart*, c. 1646 / 1650, pen and brown ink with brown wash, Rembrandt Chronology, no. 13, National Gallery of Art, Rosenwald Collection

right: Rembrandt van Rijn, *The Mill*, 1645/1648, oil on canvas, National Gallery of Art, Widener Collection

below: Rembrandt van Rijn, *The Windmill*, 1641, etching, White/Boon 1969, no. 233, National Gallery of Art, Gift of W. G. Russell Allen

3 Wind Power

It's hard to imagine the Dutch landscape without windmills. With much of the country below sea level, windmill power was used to drain the land of water so that it could be farmed. Windmills were also used to grind wheat, corn, and barley. They contributed to the country's productivity, and the Dutch were proud of this source of prosperity.

In the etching *The Windmill,* Rembrandt describes in great detail an eight-sided grain mill and nearby cottage. As a sign of national pride, people collected pictures of the local scenery, and prints such as this one were in demand.

4 Light and Shadow

Although Rembrandt made many drawings and prints of landscapes throughout his life, he created few paintings of them. *The Mill* is his largest one. It does not depict a specific place, but instead it is an imaginary scene that Rembrandt devised from his drawings. The windmill sits high on a hill, its sails full, silhouetted against a cloudy sky. Interested in the effects of changing weather, Rembrandt shows the sunlight breaking through the clouds after a storm. People around the windmill are engaged in everyday activities: a woman washes clothes at the edge of the river, a fisherman rows home, and a woman walks with her child.

The land and people are engulfed in deep shadows, while the windmill, sunlit on high ground, stands out against the sky. Rembrandt is known for his strong contrasts of light and dark. He used light to feature some areas of a picture, and he left other parts in shade. This technique, called *chiaroscuro* (from the Italian words for "light" and "dark"), can make an ordinary scene look dramatic. Rembrandt composed many of his portraits in a similar way. In his *Self-Portrait* of 1659, the light is cast on his face to draw attention to it, leaving much of his body in shadow.

Self-Portraits

Rembrandt did not paint many landscapes, but one "landscape" with which he was very familiar was the terrain of his own face. He closely studied his face and made sketches, etchings, and paintings of himself more than a hundred times. In a way, he was his favorite model. He could experiment with various techniques and practice drawing facial expressions that conveyed different feelings, such as fear, worry, melancholy, surprise, or amusement. Painted over the years, his self-portraits show him young and old, dressed in everyday clothes or wearing theatrical costumes and elegant hats. And in some, Rembrandt examines his identity as an artist.

Rembrandt was fifty-three years old when he painted the self-portrait wearing an artist's cap and a brown painter's jacket. The light illuminates his head, drawing attention to his deep-set eyes, wrinkled cheeks, and furrowed brow. To create his scruffy gray hair, Rembrandt used the end of his paintbrush handle to scratch through the wet paint to make curls. Light also accents his left shoulder and clasped hands, but most of the painting is in dark shadow. What might he be thinking and feeling?

Make a self-portrait

You will need:
A mirror
Paper
Crayons, markers, colored pencils, or paints

Making a self-portrait is a way of getting to know yourself. First, think about these questions: What makes you who you are? What are your interests? Your dreams? Select clothing that reflects something about you. You might want to include objects in your self-portrait that help describe your personality. Think of a self-portrait as a personal introduction. What do you want to tell people about yourself? How do you want people to remember you?

Next, study yourself in the mirror. What features make you unique? Try out different facial expressions—smile, frown, or laugh—and strike different poses. Do you want to look relaxed, physically active, or deep in thought? Then, try to capture your appearance and character on paper. Like Rembrandt, experiment by creating many different self-portraits. You might even wish to put yourself in a landscape or place that is special to you.

top: Rembrandt van Rijn, *Self-Portrait*, 1659, oil on canvas, National Gallery of Art, Andrew W. Mellon Collection

middle: Rembrandt van Rijn, *Self-Portrait*, c. 1637, red chalk, Rembrandt Chronology, no. 7, National Gallery of Art, Rosenwald Collection

bottom: Rembrandt van Rijn, *Self-Portrait in a Cap, Open-Mouthed*, 1630, etching, White/Boon 1969, no. 320, National Gallery of Art, Rosenwald Collection

1 Venetian Artist

Giovanni Antonio Canal (1697–1768) is best known for his painted views of his hometown: Venice, Italy. Capturing its appearance and distinctive character, his paintings transport viewers back to this famous city on the water. He was nicknamed Canaletto (the little Canal) to distinguish him from his father, who was also an artist. Canaletto specialized in topographical views—paintings that describe the landscape and architecture of a particular place. His paintings were popular because he recorded in vivid detail the appearance of the city and the diverse activities of its people. To achieve convincing realism in his scenes, Canaletto first made several sketches outside. He then took these quick drawings back to his studio, where he painted his large-scale canvases. He worked on the architecture before he added the figures on the plazas and canals. Canaletto's city views are much more than a painted "photograph": he often improved the appearance of a place, making it look better than it actually was!

2 Travel Souvenirs

In the eighteenth century, Venice became a favorite tourist destination in Europe. With its beautiful setting, many canals, and magnificent architecture, the city attracted foreign visitors who enjoyed its carnivals, regattas, festivals, and theater. Travelers wanted souvenirs of their visit to Venice. Before cameras were invented, tourists bought paintings and drawings to take home. Canaletto painted scenes of Venice often, and he built a successful career by selling his work to wealthy tourists.

3 Entrance to the Grand Canal

A large Italian port on the Adriatic Sea, Venice was an important center for trade between Asia and Europe. It also boasted a thriving fishing industry. This view shows the popular waterfront leading to the Grand Canal, the main waterway through Venice. Large oceangoing ships, including one with a British flag, have dropped their sails and are anchored to unload their cargo and tourists. Gondolas glide across the glistening water, ferrying passengers across the canals. In the center is the Customs House, where goods are unloaded and taxed. A small globe above its dome symbolizes the city's overseas trade. Groups of people gather along the dock, stop to chat with one another, and shop. Fishermen display the day's catch of eels and mussels in round wooden trays.

4 Saint Mark's Square

Located at the very heart of Venice are Saint Mark's Square and the Church of Saint Mark with its elaborate architecture, bluish domes, and shimmering mosaics. To the right is the pink marble Doge's Palace, once home to the elected rulers of Venice.

Around three bronze flagpoles, merchants set up tables, take goods out of trunks, and display bolts of cloth at booths protected by umbrellas. These activities, and the ships off in the distance, highlight Venice's role as a center of trade. Canaletto included about two hundred figures in this painting!

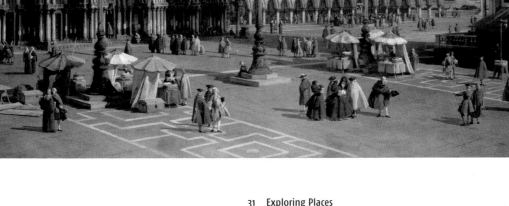

Canaletto, *The Square of Saint Mark's, Venice*, 1742/1744, oil on canvas, National Gallery of Art, Gift of Mrs. Barbara Hutton

Giovanni Paolo Panini, *Interior of Saint Peter's, Rome*, c. 1754, oil on canvas, National Gallery of Art, Ailsa Mellon Bruce Fund

This view of Saint Peter's shows off the church's large interior and elaborate architectural decorations. The worshipers and visitors provide a sense of scale and enliven the space.

Giovanni Paolo Panini, *Interior of the Pantheon, Rome*, c. 1734, oil on canvas, National Gallery of Art, Samuel H. Kress Collection

With the largest concrete dome in the world, the Pantheon has been one of the most popular monuments of classical Rome. Built as a Roman temple, it was later converted to a Christian church.

Giovanni Paolo Panini

While Canaletto was painting views of Venice, Giovanni Paolo Panini (1691–1765) was working as a "view painter" in Rome. Panini specialized in landscape and architectural views of the most famous and memorable sights of Rome, including the Pantheon and Saint Peter's Basilica at the Vatican. Similar to works by Canaletto, Panini's paintings were popular with visiting tourists, who bought them as a souvenir of their travels.

Postcard Memories

Take an imaginary trip to Italy and write a postcard to a friend.

Choose a painting by Canaletto or Panini and imagine you can "jump" into the scene. What would you do? Where would you explore? Who would you meet?

Write a postcard from this place and describe your travels. Begin with, "I visited _____ and I saw _____ ."

Create a postcard picture of your hometown

Make a postcard by cutting a piece of white cardstock or watercolor paper into a rectangle (3.5 × 5 inches or 4 × 6 inches). On one side, use colored pencils to draw a view of your hometown. Choose a well-known park, school, monument, or shopping center. Add details of the landscape, buildings, and people. Divide the other side in half. On the left side, write a note to a friend, a family member, or yourself! Share a special memory of your hometown. On the right side, write the address on the postcard, place a stamp in the upper right corner, and send it in the mail.

1 Cropsey's Colors

In the mid-nineteenth century, landscape painting grew in popularity among artists in the United States. Captivated by the sweeping vistas of their country, many of them explored and painted the picturesque valley of New York's Hudson River. One of these "Hudson River School" painters was Jasper Francis Cropsey (1823–1900).

Born on Staten Island, New York, Cropsey trained to be an architect, but his real love was painting. In the 1840s he made summer sketching trips to New Jersey, Upstate New York, Vermont, and New Hampshire. He and his wife moved to London in 1856, where they lived for seven years before returning to America.

Cropsey became best known for his paintings of autumn landscapes. His works were more than just descriptions of nature: they were patriotic celebrations of the wonders and promises of a young nation carved from the wilderness.

Jasper Francis Cropsey (detail),
Collection of Time & Life Pictures
(photo: Tony Linck)

2 Autumn on the Hudson

Painted in 1860, this monumental view of the Hudson River Valley shows a scene set about sixty miles north of New York City, between the towns of Newburgh and West Point. From a high vantage point on the west side of the Hudson River, a small stream leads to the wide expanse of the river. The distinctive profile of Storm King Mountain is off in the distance. Behind thick gray-blue clouds, the sun's piercing rays give a mellow glow to the hazy atmosphere. Celebrating the richness and variety of autumn foliage, tall, graceful trees in the foreground frame the view into the distance. Red oak, sugar maple, birch, and chestnut trees—having assumed their different shades of yellow, bronze, scarlet, and orange—are intermingled with the evergreen hemlocks and pines.

Jasper Francis Cropsey, *Autumn — On the Hudson River,* 1860, oil on canvas, National Gallery of Art, Gift of the Avalon Foundation

3 Wander into This Landscape

Autumn — On the Hudson River is a sweeping vista with precise details. The magnificent panorama, with closely observed elements, conveys an idea of the magnitude and splendor of the American landscape.

Look closely to find:

A group of hunters with their dogs

A log cabin

A winding stream

Large boulders around a pool of water

Grazing sheep

Children playing on a bridge

Cows wading in the water

Boats crossing the river

A small town nestled along the shore

Imagine you have traveled to this place

What sounds might you hear?

What might you smell?

How would you dress for this trip?

What parts of the landscape would you explore?

Where would you stand for the best view of the mountain?

What might you see from the top of a mountain?

How would this place look in the winter? In the summer?

Remarkably, Cropsey painted *Autumn — On the Hudson River* while he lived in London. He relied on his memory and on sketches he made of autumn in rural New York. Cropsey's largest painting, measuring almost nine feet wide and five feet tall, took more than a year to complete, but it was an immediate success when it was exhibited in London. The painting created a sensation among English viewers who had never seen such a colorful panorama of fall foliage. (Autumn in Britain is far less colorful than in the eastern United States because there are fewer deciduous trees.) Cropsey also displayed specimens of North American leaves alongside his painting to persuade skeptical visitors that his rendition was botanically accurate.

Celebrate Autumn!

Each season presents a new inspiration for artists. During the season of autumn, wander through your backyard, neighborhood, or a park.

Look at leaves the way an artist might.

Examine the range of colors, from bright reds, oranges, and yellows to browns and greens.

Notice the different sizes and shapes of leaves—big, small, thin, fat, round, and pointy.

Look at the textures and vein patterns of leaves.

Collect a variety of leaves that have fallen to the ground and create a work of art with them.

Leaf Rubbing

You will need:
Leaves
Plain white paper
Crayons

On a piece of plain white paper, arrange the leaves (with the vein side up) in a pattern you like.

Lay another sheet of plain white paper on top of the leaves.

Select a crayon and peel off its paper wrapper.

Using the side of the crayon, gently rub it over the top sheet of paper.

An image of the leaf will begin to appear on the paper! Experiment with different colors and leaf arrangements.

Leaf Collage

You will need:
Leaves
Newspaper
Rubber cement
Paper
Clear contact paper

Clean the leaves you've collected by rinsing them in warm water. Carefully blot them dry with a paper towel.

Place the leaves between sheets of newspaper, and then put them between two heavy books. In about a week, the dried leaves should be flat and stiff.

Arrange the dried leaves in an interesting design on a piece of paper. Use rubber cement to glue them in place.

Let the rubber cement dry for one day. To protect the surface, cover your collage with clear contact paper.

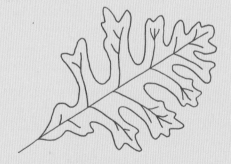

"Have you ever reclined upon some gentle slope, some hillside in a beautiful country with your eyes half closed and your mind away from care, dreaming of . . . the lovely and beautiful in nature and art with a far away and o'er the hills feeling of the chameleon sky, the glowing sunshine and soothing shadows — the distant smoky town — the rich autumnal foliage, bits of green pasturage and nibbling sheep and stately trees, a stream of water winding in and out around some wooded headland. . . ." Jasper Francis Cropsey

1 Painter of the American West

Born in England, Thomas Moran (1837–1926) grew up near Philadelphia after his parents moved to the United States in 1844. A promising young artist, he served as an apprentice in Philadelphia and then traveled to Europe, where he was influenced by the work of the British landscape painter J.M.W. Turner. An avid traveler, Moran spent his long career painting diverse landscapes, from Pennsylvania and Long Island to Arizona, Idaho, Colorado, Wyoming, Utah, Montana, California, and even Cuba, Mexico, and Italy. He became famous for his paintings of Western territories. They were received with great enthusiasm by a public who saw westward expansion as a symbol of hope for America.

Moran's adventures in the West began in 1871. Just a few months earlier a magazine publisher asked him to illustrate an article about Yellowstone, a wondrous region of the Wyoming Territory that was rumored to have steam-spewing geysers, boiling hot springs, and bubbling mud pots. Eager to be the first artist to record these astonishing natural wonders, Moran quickly made plans to travel west.

He joined geologist Ferdinand V. Hayden on the first government-sponsored survey expedition of Yellowstone Valley. This area, while virtually unknown, was a source of great interest and curiosity. Hayden's goal was to map and measure Yellowstone, and Moran's role was to record the scenery of the region. The artist made many watercolor sketches, which became the first color pictures of Yellowstone seen in the eastern United States.

2 Colorful Cliffs

Yellowstone was Moran's ultimate destination in the summer of 1871, but before he joined Hayden's expedition, the artist stepped off the train in Green River, Wyoming, and discovered a landscape unlike any he had ever seen. Rising above the dusty railroad town were towering cliffs of sandstone carved by centuries of wind and water. Captivated by the bands of color, Moran made his first sketches of the American West.

Over the years, Moran repeatedly painted the magnificent cliffs of Green River, the western landscape he saw first. *Green River Cliffs, Wyoming* was painted in 1881, ten years after his first trip west. Moran referred to his sketches in his studio, but he also took some artistic license since he believed it was better to express the distinct character of the region than it was to record a view with strict accuracy. Green River was a busy railroad town when Moran arrived in 1871, yet no indication of the town — the Union Pacific Railroad, hotel, church, schoolhouse, and brewery — is seen. Instead, the dazzling colors of the sculpted mountains and a caravan of American Indians are the focus. Moran erased the reality of commercial development and replaced it with an imagined scene of the pre-industrial West that neither he nor anyone else could have seen in 1871.

3 Preserving America's Beauty

Soon after Moran returned to the East, Hayden and others began promoting the idea that Yellowstone should be protected and preserved. Since no member of Congress had seen Yellowstone, Moran's watercolors played a key role in the congressional decision to pass the bill creating the first national park, which established Yellowstone National Park and the national park system. Mount Moran in the Grand Teton Mountains was named for the artist in honor of his role in preserving America's wilderness.

Yellowstone was just the beginning for Moran. He made numerous trips to the West, painting scenes of the Grand Canyon, Yosemite Valley, the Grand Tetons, Colorado's Mountain of the Holy Cross, and the Snake River. Moran's works sparked the American imagination and helped the national parks become popular tourist destinations.

above: Thomas Moran, *Green River Cliffs, Wyoming*, 1881, oil on canvas, National Gallery of Art, Gift of the Milligan and Thomson Families

top left: Photographic portrait (detail) of the American artist Thomas Moran by Napoleon Sarony, c. 1890–1896. Photogravure (photomechanical) print. Image courtesy of the Prints and Photographs Division, Library of Congress, Washington, DC

bottom left: Thomas Moran, *Mountain of the Holy Cross*, 1890, watercolor and gouache over graphite on paper, National Gallery of Art, Avalon Fund, Florian Carr Fund, Barbara and Jack Kay Fund, Gift of Max and Heidi Berry and Veverka Family Foundation Fund

"I have always held that the Grandest, Most Beautiful, and Wonderful in Nature, would, in capable hands, make the grandest, most beautiful, or wonderful pictures, and that the business of a great painter should be the representation of great scenes in nature." **Thomas Moran to Ferdinand Hayden, March 11, 1872**

above: George Catlin, *The White Cloud, Head Chief of the Iowas*, 1844/1845, oil on canvas, National Gallery of Art, Paul Mellon Collection

top right: George Catlin, *A Buffalo Wallow*, 1861/1869, oil on card mounted on paperboard, National Gallery of Art, Paul Mellon Collection

For many tribes on the Great Plains, buffalo were an important source of food, clothes, cooking pots, and tools.

George Catlin

Like Moran, George Catlin (1796–1872) became famous for his paintings of the American West. Born in Pennsylvania, Catlin first trained to be a lawyer, and he enjoyed sketching the judges, jurors, and defendants he encountered on the job. Soon he decided to become a portrait painter. After seeing a delegation of Plains Indians in Philadelphia, he dedicated himself to recording the lives and customs of American Indians. He wanted to document their way of life—people at work and play, families, leaders, and the landscape where they lived—before it vanished. Catlin spent many years traveling with different tribes, and he kept a detailed diary of his journeys. He created more than five hundred paintings. After his extensive travels, he put his paintings on view alongside American Indian artifacts in an exhibition he called *The Indian Gallery*. To educate viewers about this disappearing culture, he took the collection on tour to several cities on the East Coast and then to London.

White Cloud: Head Chief of the Iowas

Mew-hu-she-kaw, known as White Cloud or No Heart-of-Fear, was one of several tribal chiefs of the Iowa people in the mid-nineteenth century. This portrait shows not only the traditional dress of the Iowas but also the chief's important status within the tribe and his brave nature. He wears a white wolf skin over the shoulders of his deerskin shirt, strands of beads and carved conch shell tubes in his pierced ears, and a headdress made of a deer's tail (dyed vermillion) and eagle's quills above a turban of (possibly otter) fur. His face is painted red and marked with green handprints, a sign that he was very good at hand-to-hand fighting. The necklace of bear claws testifies to his skill, because it was reserved for those who earned success as hunters and warriors. Catlin admired the American Indian people, and his portraits emphasize their dignity and pride.

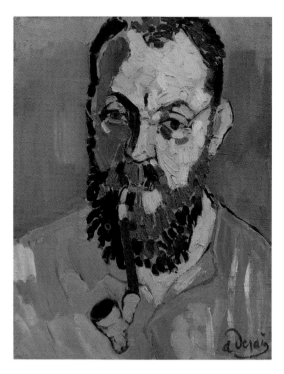

1 Summer in the Sun

Artists often leave their studios and travel to new places for inspiration. In the summer of 1905, Henri Matisse (1869–1954) left Paris for the French village of Collioure. Then a quiet fishing town, Collioure nestles between the Mediterranean Sea and the Pyrenees Mountains close to the Spanish border. The landscape and lifestyle there were very different from Paris. The brilliant light in the south of France, reflected off the sea, captivated Matisse.

above: André Derain, *Portrait of Henri Matisse,* 1905, oil on canvas, Tate Gallery, London, Great Britain © ARS, NY. Photo credit: Tate, London / Art Resource, NY

right: Henri Matisse, *André Derain,* 1905, oil on canvas, Tate Gallery, London, Great Britain © Succession H. Matisse, Paris / ARS, NY. Photo credit: Tate, London / Art Resource, NY

"We were always intoxicated with color, with words that speak of color, and with the sun that makes colors live." André Derain

2 Side by Side

After settling with his family in a hotel, Matisse invited his friend, the young painter André Derain (1880–1954), to join him in Collioure. Matisse and Derain worked every day, often painting side by side around the village. They sketched the boats in the harbor, the fish market, and the nearby Pyrenees. They even made pictures of each other. Using paints straight from the tube with little mixing of pigments, they applied vibrant—often unexpected—colors directly to their canvases. Their collaboration led to a new freedom in creating art: the use of color to express the feeling of a place.

3 The Wild Beasts

In the fall of 1905, Matisse and Derain showed their paintings at an important exhibition in Paris called the Salon d'automne. People were shocked by the bold brushstrokes and strange color combinations. Many laughed at the paintings. One art critic nicknamed the artists *fauves* (the French word for "wild beasts") because of their expressive brushstrokes and loud colors. Matisse and Derain inspired many artists to explore color in new ways.

Two Views of Collioure

Matisse and Derain do not show Collioure as it looked in real life. Instead, the artists conveyed the intensity and energy of Collioure's blazing sunshine by painting with dazzling colors.

Look at *Open Window, Collioure,* Matisse's view of the town port. Visible through the window, small boats bob on pink waves under a sky banded with turquoise, pink, and periwinkle. Vibrant outdoor light pours through the window and onto the flower pots on the sill, coloring the windows mauve, azure, and pink.

Turning from the sea in *Mountains at Collioure,* Derain painted the olive groves with the steep hills of the Pyrenees in the background. Notice how Derain used a variety of brushstrokes to paint this rugged landscape. Examine how the twisting red lines form the trunks of the olive trees. Derain's bold, separated stripes of blues, grays, and greens create a rhythmic pattern of leaves ready to wave in a breeze. Broad, sweeping strokes of color form the mountains rising behind the trees and reaching to the sky.

"When I realized that every morning I would see this light again, I couldn't believe how lucky I was." **Henri Matisse**

top: Henri Matisse, *Open Window, Collioure,* 1905, oil on canvas, National Gallery of Art, Collection of Mr. and Mrs. John Hay Whitney

bottom: André Derain, *Mountains at Collioure,* 1905, oil on canvas, National Gallery of Art, John Hay Whitney Collection

Colorful Cut-Outs

Matisse enjoyed staying in warmer places during the winter months, and he liked to watch sunlight shimmering on the sea. After his summer with Derain, he returned to Collioure and vacationed at other seaports on the French coast of the Mediterranean Sea. He also visited Italy, North Africa, and Tahiti. *Beasts of the Sea* is a memory of his visit to the South Seas.

Many years after creating his *fauve* paintings, Matisse developed a new form of art: the paper cut-out. Still fascinated by the power of color, the artist devoted himself to cutting painted papers and arranging them in designs. "Instead of drawing an outline and filling in the color... I am drawing directly in color," he said. Matisse was drawing with scissors!

What shapes do you recognize in *Beasts of the Sea*? Find shapes that remind you of

After cutting shapes that reminded him of a tropical sea, Matisse arranged the pieces vertically over rectangles of yellows, greens, and purples to suggest the watery depths of an undersea world.

Create a colorful collage

Use colored papers, or like Matisse, make your own colored paper by painting entire sheets of white paper in one color. Paint on heavy cardstock so the paper doesn't curl as it dries. Next, find a theme for your work. Like Matisse, choose a view from your window or a memory from vacation. Use scissors to cut the paper into different shapes that remind you of that place. Arrange your cut-out shapes on a large piece of colored paper. Move the pieces around and experiment with layering until you are satisfied with the design, then glue your shapes in place.

While creating the cut-outs, Matisse hung them on the walls and ceiling of his apartment in Nice, France. "Thanks to my new art, I have a lush garden all around me. And I am never alone," he said.

les bêtes de la mer...
h. matisse 50

above: Henri Matisse, *Beasts of the Sea*, 1950, paper collage on canvas, National Gallery of Art, Ailsa Mellon Bruce Fund

top right: Henri Matisse at work on a paper cut-out in his studio at the Hôtel Régina, early 1952, Nice-Cimiez. Hélène Adant (20th c.) © Copyright Photographic Archive. The Museum of Modern Art Archives, New York. Digital Image © The Museum of Modern Art/Licensed by SCALA/Art Resource, NY. The Museum of Modern Art, New York, NY, U.S.A.

playful fish

sinuous eels

floating seahorses

curvy coral

spiral shells

waving seaweed

George Bellows, c. 1900, Peter A. Juley & Son Collection. Smithsonian American Art Museum

1 Bellows' New York

Throughout his childhood in Columbus, Ohio, George Bellows (1882–1925) divided much of his time between art and sports. While attending Ohio State University, he created illustrations for the school yearbooks, sang in the glee club, and played basketball and baseball. Bellows left college before graduating, and even turned down an offer to play professional baseball with the Cincinnati Reds, all because he wanted to become an artist.

In 1904 Bellows left the Midwest for Manhattan, where he enrolled in the New York School of Art. There he studied under the well-known teacher and artist Robert Henri, who encouraged students to be inspired by real life: "Draw your material from the life around you, from all of it. There is beauty in everything if it looks beautiful to your eyes." Bellows became linked with a group of artists who were also inspired by Henri. Critics dubbed them the Ashcan School due to the way they showed the grittier side of life in the city.

Bellows' early paintings focused on dynamic city scenes: busy streets, boxing matches, construction sites, commercial docks, and poor neighborhoods. He eventually expanded his subjects to include seascapes, country scenes, and portraits of friends and family. His work met with popular success during his lifetime. Bellows died at age forty-two from a ruptured appendix.

2 Traffic Jam!

Bellows captured the whirlwind of activity on a winter day in his painting *New York*. The picture is a congestion of buildings, signage, and people and goods on the move. Motorcars mingle with horse-drawn conveyances and trolleys while pedestrians hurry along sidewalks. When Bellows created this work in 1911, the traffic light had not yet been invented. In the painting you can see a policeman trying to direct traffic, a street cleaner busy sweeping, and a woman stopping at a vegetable cart. Bellows' use of expressive brushstrokes adds to the energy of the scene.

George Bellows, *New York*, 1911, oil on canvas, National Gallery of Art, Collection of Mr. and Mrs. Paul Mellon

"Some day far in the future it will be pointed out, no doubt, as the best description of the casual New York scene left by the reporters of the present day."
New York Times, 1911

Although the painting's general location is Madison Square at the intersection of Broadway and Twenty-third Street, Bellows imaginatively combined elements that could not be seen from a single viewpoint. Many of Manhattan's most famous features are seen: skyscrapers, apartment buildings, elevated train tracks, a subway entrance, electric signs, advertising billboards, and a tree-lined park. Although these features are familiar today, they represented an exciting, modern experience for most people at the beginning of the twentieth century.

3 Construction Zone

In the early twentieth century, New York was changing into a metropolis with vast building projects that included new bridges and skyscrapers. Construction of the Pennsylvania Railroad Station took place from 1906 to 1910. This complex endeavor required tearing down entire blocks of old buildings, digging giant pits, and boring several sets of large tunnels under the Hudson and East rivers. The energy, drama, and scope of the engineering project fascinated Bellows, and he began a series of paintings to study construction scenes by day and night, in summer and winter.

Blue Morning shows the nearly completed station enveloped in morning haze. Construction workers are busy in the excavated pit; a crane arm rises. The elevated train tracks and a vertical girder frame the scene. Bellows used tones of blue, lavender, and yellow to create a sense of the morning light.

George Bellows, *Blue Morning*, 1909, oil on canvas, National Gallery of Art, Chester Dale Collection

"Be deliberate. Be spontaneous. Be thoughtful, and painstaking. Be abandoned, and impulsive. Learn your own possibilities." **George Bellows**

"I paint New York because I live in it and because the most essential thing for me to paint is the life about me, the things I feel to-day and that are part of the life of to-day." George Bellows

George Bellows, *The Lone Tenement*, 1909, oil on canvas, National Gallery of Art, Chester Dale Collection

Capturing Urban Life

The Lone Tenement is set under the Queensboro Bridge, which was completed in 1909 to connect the boroughs of Manhattan and Queens. Dwarfed by the newly constructed bridge, the last remaining row house stands alone, the sole survivor of its former busy neighborhood. People gather around a fire to keep warm in the shadow of the bridge. Sunlight sparkles on the East River as a ship passes by. Instead of celebrating the bridge as an engineering accomplishment, Bellows focuses on the lives of ordinary people who were affected by its construction.

Documenting Changing Times

Many artists in the early twentieth century, including Bellows, worked as sketch reporters. In an era before the widespread use of photography, they drew illustrations for newspapers and magazines as a way to document events in the city. Along with many of the Ashcan School artists, Bellows was concerned about the social issues of his time, including poverty and the way large building projects changed neighborhoods.

Write a headline

Write a news story headline (for a newspaper, magazine, or website) for each of the paintings by Bellows in this section. Summarize the main idea of each picture in an interesting way to catch people's attention.

Be a sketch reporter

Choose a headline or news story from a newspaper, magazine, or television report. Make a drawing or painting that illustrates the story. Capture the key points of the story in one picture.

What places excite
your creativity?

examining portraits

Portraits can describe a person's physical likeness, status, personality, and/or interests. This chapter presents the range of ways artists represent people. Discover a rare double-sided portrait by Leonardo da Vinci. Rich and powerful aristocrats and royalty had their portraits painted by the French artist Élisabeth-Louise Vigée Le Brun, and the emperor Napoleon posed for Jacques-Louis David. Introspective and enigmatic, Vincent van Gogh and Paul Gauguin painted self-portraits that express their personal styles, while Chuck Close creates large-scale portraits with surprising and innovative techniques. As you examine the works in this chapter, consider what portraits reveal about the sitter and what they tell us about the artist.

1 Who Was Ginevra?

Ginevra d'Amerigo de' Benci (1457– c. 1520) lived in Florence, Italy, five hundred years ago. The daughter of a wealthy banker, she was the second of seven children. Her nickname, La Bencina ("little Benci"), was likely an endearing reference to her delicate appearance and gentle spirit. Ginevra was a poet (although only a single line of her work survives), and she was praised by those who knew her for her intellect and virtuous character. Leonardo painted her portrait around the time she married in 1474.

Ginevra was about sixteen years old in this portrait. It presents her as a refined young woman with a porcelain complexion. Her modest brown dress is enlivened with elegant details: blue ribbon lacing, gold edging, and a sheer white blouse fastened with a delicate gold pin or button. A black scarf is gently draped over her slender shoulders and neck. Her golden hair is styled simply—parted in the middle and pulled back in a bun—leaving ringlets to frame her face. Without the distractions of luxurious fabrics and sparkling gems, Ginevra herself attracts attention. Her brown eyes gaze steadily from under almond-shaped lids, and her lips are closed in a quiet line. Unlike portraits in profile that were more typical at the time, Ginevra's portrait shows her in a three-quarter view as a way to reveal more about her.

Describe Ginevra's expression. How does she feel? What might she be thinking about? What aspects of her personality does the portrait convey?

"A face is not well done unless it expresses a state of mind." Leonardo da Vinci

2 A Renaissance Man

Italian artist Leonardo da Vinci (1452–1519) lived during an exciting period known as the Renaissance (French for "rebirth"), a time recognized for a renewed interest in knowledge, the arts, and science. He was an artist as well as an inventor, architect, engineer, musician, mathematician, astronomer, and scientist. In many ways, his intellectual curiosity, careful observation of nature, and artistic creativity characterized the Renaissance itself.

Born in the small town of Vinci, outside Florence, Leonardo moved to the city at the age of twelve to train in the workshop of Andrea del Verrocchio, a leading artist of the time. Leonardo was just twenty-two years old when he painted this portrait of Ginevra de' Benci. It is the first of only three known portraits Leonardo painted in his career. The portrait may have been commissioned by Ginevra's older brother Giovanni on the occasion of her engagement.

Throughout his life, Leonardo embraced opportunities to experiment with materials and explore artistic approaches. Ginevra's portrait was among his earliest encounters with the medium of oil paint. Leonardo used his fingers and the palm of his hand to mix the wet paint, which enabled him to blend colors and create soft, delicate edges that allowed for subtle transitions from light to shadow. Evidence of Leonardo's innovative technique remains on the painting: his fingerprint is visible on the surface, where the sky meets the juniper bush above Ginevra's left shoulder.

3

A Landscape Painting, Too?

This was among the first portraits created in Florence that showed a sitter outdoors. In fact, Leonardo gave almost as much attention to the landscape as he did to Ginevra. Behind her is a tranquil scene with small trees lining the banks of a pool of water and a town nestled in the hills under a misty sky.

The large plant behind Ginevra's head is a juniper bush, an evergreen with sharp, spiky leaves. It is a witty pun on Ginevra's name: *ginepro* is the Italian word for juniper.

Both the figure and the landscape have been praised for their lifelike appearance. The painting demonstrates Leonardo's careful observation of the natural world, a practice he continued throughout his career that came to transform Renaissance painting.

4

Something's Missing!

Leonardo's original portrait probably included Ginevra's waist and hands. It was rectangular in shape instead of square and painted on a wood panel that was originally larger than what is seen today. At some point—possibly because of water damage—about six inches of the panel were cut off along the bottom and the right edge was trimmed.

Imagine how the portrait might have looked originally
How might Ginevra's hands have been posed? What would the rest of her dress look like?

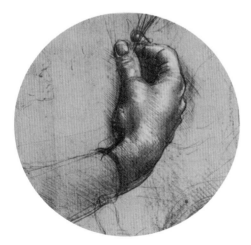

left: Leonardo da Vinci, *Study of female hands* (detail), drawing, Royal Library, Windsor Castle, Windsor, Great Britain. Photo credit: Alinari/Art Resource, NY

above: Leonardo da Vinci, *Ginevra de' Benci*, c. 1474/1478, oil on panel, National Gallery of Art, Ailsa Mellon Bruce Fund

Dotted line shows probable size of original portrait.

A Double-sided Portrait

In addition to the front side of the portrait, Leonardo was asked to create an image on its reverse. On this "verso" side, Leonardo painted a scroll entwined around a wreath of laurel and palm branches, with a sprig of juniper in the center. While the front of the painting is a physical portrait of Ginevra, the reverse is an emblematic portrait: it uses symbols to describe her personality. The juniper sprig identifies Ginevra by name, and the laurel and palm branches represent two of her attributes: intelligence and strong moral values. The scroll bears a Latin inscription: *virtutem forma decorat.* This translates as Beauty Adorns Virtue, which was Ginevra's motto.

Originally, this painting might have hung from a ring on a wall or a piece of furniture so one side or the other could be seen. Today the painting is displayed in a free-standing case that shows both sides of the panel. It is thought to be Leonardo's only double-sided painting.

Imagine what your own emblematic portrait might include (words, symbols, and so on).

Think about what you would illustrate about yourself. Which of your personality traits do you want people to remember? What characteristics make you unique?

Share these ideas with a family member or friend.

Create a double-sided self-portrait, with one side showing your physical appearance and the other side presenting an emblem of your personality and/or interests.

Leonardo da Vinci, *Wreath of Laurel, Palm, and Juniper with a Scroll inscribed Virtutem Forma Decorat* (reverse), c. 1474 / 1478, tempera on panel, National Gallery of Art, Ailsa Mellon Bruce Fund

It is believed Prince Carl Eusebius of Liechtenstein purchased this painting after 1611. The red wax seal on the upper right corner of the panel was added in 1733, when the painting was inventoried as part of the collection of Prince Joseph Wenzel of Liechtenstein. *Ginevra de' Benci* was purchased from Prince Franz Joseph II of Liechtenstein for the National Gallery's collection in 1967.

1 Pleasing Portraits

Élisabeth-Louise Vigée Le Brun (1755–1842) was so successful as a portrait painter in France during the late eighteenth century that she often had a waiting list! Why was she so popular? She pleased her clients by making them look attractive, with graceful poses and happy expressions. Her works mirrored fashionable life before the French Revolution of 1789.

Today Vigée Le Brun is known especially for her paintings of women and children. This group portrait depicts two of the artist's close friends: the Marquise de Pezay, in the blue gown, and the Marquise de Rougé, the mother of the two young boys. The older boy, Alexis, gazes lovingly at his mother as he hugs her tightly, while the younger boy, Adrien, rests his head in her lap. Adrien wears a dress, which was typical for young boys at the time.

Élisabeth-Louise Vigée Le Brun, *The Marquise de Pezay and the Marquise de Rougé with Her Sons Alexis and Adrien*, 1787, oil on canvas, National Gallery of Art, Gift of the Bay Foundation in memory of Josephine Bay Paul and Ambassador Charles Ulrick Bay

Élisabeth-Louise Vigée Le Brun, *Madame d'Aguesseau de Fresnes*, 1789, oil on wood, National Gallery of Art, Samuel H. Kress Collection

2 Style and Skill

Vigée Le Brun was interested in fashion, and she painted clothing with great detail and brilliant technique. She showed off her sitters' wealth and elegance by depicting their luxurious garments and expensive accessories.

Imagine the textures of the fabric—the shimmering silks and iridescent taffetas of the flowing dresses worn by the Marquise de Pezay and the Marquise de Rougé. In another portrait, she meticulously painted the small embroidered gold circles on the white chiffon skirt of Madame d'Aguesseau de Fresnes. Vigée Le Brun carefully observed details, such as lace or gold edging, and she often selected her sitters' attire. She even designed imaginative headdresses inspired by turbans from the Ottoman Empire.

3 Painter to the Queen

Vigée Le Brun was born in Paris during the reign of Louis XV. Her father, an artist, introduced her to painting, but he died when she was just twelve years old. Mainly self-taught, Vigée Le Brun became a portrait painter to support her mother and brother. Talented and hard-working, she soon earned critical and financial success. She married an art dealer, and they had one daughter. In 1778 Vigée Le Brun was summoned to Versailles, the palace of King Louis XVI and Queen Marie-Antoinette. She became the queen's favorite painter, and the two women were soon friends.

This was a time of political turmoil in France. Most of the common people resented the extravagant lifestyles of the noble classes. Finally, the tense situation exploded into the French Revolution, which brought ten years of violence. Many of Vigée Le Brun's friends and patrons, including King Louis XVI and Queen Marie-Antoinette, were beheaded. As an artist associated with the royal court, Vigée Le Brun was also in danger, and she fled Paris in disguise. She spent the next sixteen years traveling in Italy, Germany, Austria, Russia, and England while painting portraits of wealthy families and royalty. Vigée Le Brun finally returned to France in 1805, after Napoleon Bonaparte had established a new empire and the revolution ended. She continued painting and was even asked to create a portrait of Napoleon's sister. A celebrity in her own lifetime, Vigée Le Brun painted more than eight hundred portraits.

After Élisabeth-Louise Vigée Le Brun, *Marie-Antoinette*, after 1783, oil on canvas, National Gallery of Art, Timken Collection

another view

Jacques-Louis David

Napoleon Bonaparte became the ruler of France in 1799 and crowned himself emperor in 1804. The artist Jacques-Louis David (1748–1825) painted this portrait when Napoleon was forty-three years old. Appointed by Napoleon to the important position of "First Painter," David created many portraits of the ruler and depicted significant events during his reign. His paintings celebrated the emperor's accomplishments, helped people become familiar with his policies, and played a large role in shaping the image of Napoleon as the new leader of France.

This nearly life-size portrait shows Napoleon in his study at the Tuileries palace. He appears to have just risen from his desk, rumpling the carpet as he pushed back his chair. Although it seems to be a casual, spontaneous picture of Napoleon at work, it is a precisely planned composition designed to convey a message about the emperor. Study the painting's details. They provide clues that tell us Napoleon wanted to be identified with qualities of strength, leadership, and public service.

Two years after David completed this painting, Napoleon was defeated in battle and overthrown as emperor. David was banished from France due to his loyalty to Napoleon, and the artist spent the remaining years of his career in Brussels, Belgium.

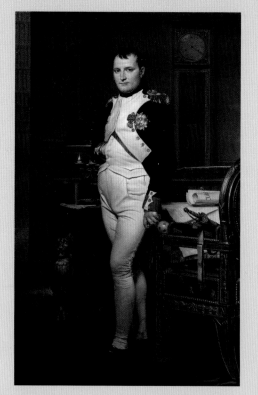

Jacques-Louis David, *The Emperor Napoleon in His Study at the Tuileries*, 1812, oil on canvas, National Gallery of Art, Samuel H. Kress Collection

Military Leader

- Napoleon wears the blue, white, and red uniform of a general in the French military. This reminds viewers that he was the commander of the troops.

- A gold-handled sword rests nearby, another symbol of his military power.

- A half-rolled map used for military plans is on the floor, behind the left side of the desk. (David placed his name on it as a way of signing and dating his painting.)

- On the floor under the desk is the book *Lives* by Plutarch. It contains biographies of Julius Caesar, Hannibal, and other powerful generals. This suggests Napoleon is continuing their tradition of military greatness.

Lawmaker

- The rolled paper on the desk with the letters C O D E refers to the Napoleonic Code, a new system of laws for the people of France.

Hard Worker

- The clock reads 4:13. Has Napoleon been working all night?

- The candles on the desk have burned almost completely down, another indication that he's been at his desk for several hours.

- The fabric on the chair is decorated with gold bees and the letter N of his imperial emblem. The bees suggest the emperor is industrious, diligent, and works tirelessly for the people of France.

"By night I work for the welfare of my people, and by day, for their glory."
Napoleon Bonaparte

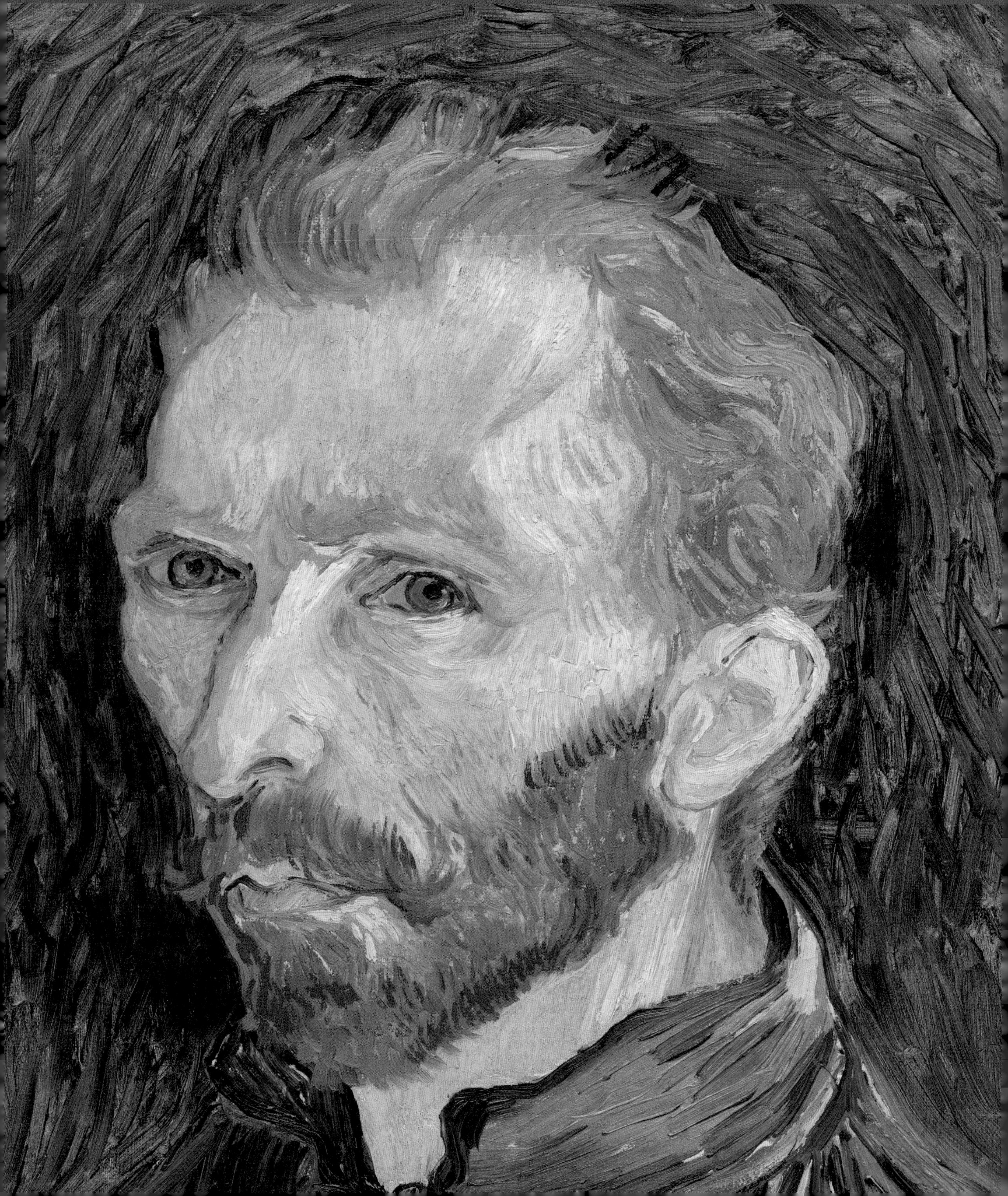

1 A Rocky Friendship

Vincent van Gogh (1853–1890) and Paul Gauguin (1848–1903) both experimented with the expressive possibilities of color and line to create distinct personal styles of painting. Working in France at the end of the nineteenth century, the two friends inspired each other during a nine-week period in the autumn of 1888.

In February of that year, Van Gogh moved to the peaceful town of Arles in the south of France. He dreamed of creating a "studio of the south" where a group of artists could work and live as a community. He invited his friend and fellow painter Gauguin to join him. Van Gogh transformed his yellow house into an artist's studio in anticipation. Gauguin finally moved to Arles in October of 1888. Although they learned from each other's techniques and produced many works side by side, Van Gogh's stubborn nature and Gauguin's pride and arrogance made their life together difficult. After nine weeks, a passionate argument caused Van Gogh to have a mental breakdown, and Gauguin returned to Paris. Despite the unhappy ending to the "studio of the south," the two painters remained friends, and they wrote letters to each other until Van Gogh died two years later.

Even though they had different personalities, the two artists shared some things in common:

Both were essentially self-taught artists.

They both left city life in Paris in search of nature.

Both admired the brilliant color, simplified forms, and unconventional compositions of Japanese prints.

Each painted a variety of subjects, including landscapes, still lifes, and portraits.

Neither achieved fame until after his death, yet their works greatly influenced twentieth-century artists.

Although Van Gogh and Gauguin were influenced by impressionism, they were not satisfied with merely capturing the visual effects of nature and instead sought to create meaning beyond surface appearances, that is, to paint with emotion and intellect as well as with the eye.

These self-portraits, painted in the year after Gauguin and Van Gogh lived together, provide a glimpse into their complex personalities and unique painting styles.

"They say — and I am very willing to believe it — that it is difficult to know yourself — but it isn't easy to paint yourself either." Vincent van Gogh, letter to Theo van Gogh, September 1889

2 A Colorful Expressionist

After Van Gogh and Gauguin quarreled in 1888, Van Gogh became ill and spent many months recuperating in a hospital. This is the first self-portrait he created after he recovered. Van Gogh chose to paint himself wearing a blue painter's smock over a white shirt and holding several paintbrushes and a palette. He was clearly asserting his identity as an artist, yet he also used intense colors to express his mood and feelings. He painted his gaunt face with yellow and green tones, and he set his vivid reddish-orange hair and beard

"For most I shall be an enigma, but for few I shall be a poet." Paul Gauguin

3 The Mysterious Symbolist

Gauguin painted this self-portrait on a panel of a cupboard door in the dining room of the inn where he was staying in Brittany, France. Around his floating head, Gauguin arranged a golden halo, two apples, a dark blue snake, and a curling vine — objects that served as personal symbols of the artist's mysterious, mystical world. Gauguin stated he had a "dual nature" and used the halo and snake to hint at his saintly and devilish sides. The apples allude to temptation.

Like Van Gogh, Gauguin manipulated color, line, and form to explore their expressive potential. His technique, however, was different. Instead of using energetic brushstrokes and thick paint, Gauguin applied his pigments thinly in smooth, flat patches of color, and outlined these broad areas of pure color with dark paint. He simplified shapes to the point of abstraction.

"Instead of trying to reproduce what I see before me, I use color in a completely arbitrary way to express myself powerfully." Vincent van Gogh, letter to Theo van Gogh, August 1888

against a deep violet-blue background. In a letter to his brother Theo, the artist described himself as looking "as thin and pale as a ghost" on the day he painted this portrait.

Known for the way he applied paint thickly, Van Gogh gives a rich texture to the canvas by leaving each brushstroke visible as opposed to blending or smoothing them. He experimented with a variety of brushstrokes — dots, dashes, curves, squiggly lines, radiating patterns, woven colors, choppy short lines, and longer rhythmic strokes — that create a sense of energy in his work.

far left: Vincent van Gogh, *Self-Portrait*, 1889, oil on canvas, National Gallery of Art, Collection of Mr. and Mrs. John Hay Whitney

left: Paul Gauguin, *Self-Portrait*, 1889, oil on wood, National Gallery of Art, Chester Dale Collection

explore more

Portraying the French Countryside

Many artists are inspired by visiting new, exciting places. Both Vincent van Gogh and Paul Gauguin left the city, seeking to renew themselves as artists in simpler, rural environments.

Compare these two landscapes. How are they similar? How are they different?

Gauguin in Brittany

In 1886 Gauguin first traveled to Brittany, a remote region of northwestern France famous for its Celtic heritage and rugged landscape. Gauguin painted *Haystacks in Brittany* in 1890. He simplified the landscape—fields, farm, haystacks, cow, and cowherd—into flat bands of color created with blocks of contrasting colors. Ever restless, Gauguin eventually found even Brittany to be too civilized. He left for Tahiti, an island in the Pacific Ocean, in 1891. Except for a brief return to France, he spent the rest of his life in French Polynesia.

Van Gogh in Provence

In the winter of 1888, Van Gogh moved to Arles in the southern region of France known as Provence. There, the dazzling sunlight, golden wheat fields, and blooming sunflowers were far different from any place Van Gogh had experienced. He was inspired by the beauty of the landscape, and he often painted outdoors to capture the bright colors and intense sunshine.

Summer was Van Gogh's favorite season, and he made many paintings depicting wheat fields and farms during the harvest. In *Farmhouse in Provence*, painted in the summer of 1888, haystacks are piled high behind a stone gate, and a farmer walks through the tall grass toward a farmhouse. The golden field seems to shimmer in the sunlight. Van Gogh energized his paintings by pairing complementary colors—the blue mountains on the horizon with yellow-orange haystacks and rooftop; the pink-purple clouds with the blue sky; the red and green flowering plants—to convey the heat of the strong southern sun.

"Don't copy nature too closely. Art is an abstraction; as you dream amid nature, extrapolate art from it."
Paul Gauguin

1 Facing Challenges

American artist Chuck Close (born 1940) is famous for painting giant portrait heads. He's also well known for facing some big challenges in his life.

Growing up, Close had severe learning disabilities that made it difficult for him to read. His talent for drawing and painting helped him to compensate for his academic struggles. He impressed his teachers by creating elaborate art projects to show he really was interested in his school subjects.

In 1988, when he was almost fifty years old, Close suffered a severe spinal artery collapse. As a result, he has only partial use of his arms and legs, and he has to rely on a wheelchair. He now uses a chair lift and motorized easel that raises, lowers, and turns the canvas to allow him to work on all parts of a painting.

Chuck Close, *Self-Portrait/ Photogravure*, 2004/2005, photogravure on Somerset Textured white, National Gallery of Art, Gift of Graphicstudio/ University of South Florida

"Almost every decision I've made as an artist is an outcome of my particular learning disorders. I'm overwhelmed by the whole. How do you make a big head? How do you make a nose? I'm not sure! But by breaking the image down into small units, I make each decision into a bite-size decision. I don't have to reinvent the wheel every day. It's an ongoing process. The system liberates and allows for intuition. And, eventually I have a painting." **Chuck Close**

Chuck Close, *Fanny*, 1984, polaroid photograph mounted on board with masking tape border; squared in ink for transfer, National Gallery of Art, Ailsa Mellon Bruce Fund

At 8 ½ by 7 feet, the painting of *Fanny* is more than five times larger than the photograph.

2 Friends and Family

Chuck Close paints close-up views of his family and friends. Every detail, every wrinkle, every strand of hair is magnified. People in Close's portraits don't show much expression or personality, much like a passport or driver's license photo.

Fanny / Fingerpainting depicts Fanny Lieber, the artist's grandmother-in-law. Fanny was the only member of her large family to survive the Holocaust, and Close admired her strength and optimism.

Chuck Close, *Fanny / Finger-painting*, 1985, oil on canvas, National Gallery of Art, Gift of Lila Acheson Wallace

3 How Does He Do It?

Close typically starts with a photograph. Instead of asking someone to sit in front of him while he paints, a slow process that could take days or months, Close takes several photographs of his subject. He then carefully selects one photo. He uses a grid to divide it into smaller units and to maintain the proportional scale between the photo and the much larger canvas. Often applying a grid to the canvas as well, he transfers the image square by square from photo to canvas. It's an exacting and painstaking process that Close has used throughout his career.

Although Close continues to employ his photo-grid process, he always looks for new challenges. At different times he has experimented with an airbrush, colored pencils, watercolor, fragments of pulp paper, printing inks, and oil and acrylic paints to create his portraits. He even used fingerprints! For *Fanny / Fingerpainting,* Close applied the paint to the canvas with his fingers, pressing harder to apply more pigment and pressing lightly for less. He placed fingerprints densely in some places and more sparingly in other areas. From a distance, the painting looks like a black-and-white photograph; up close her face dissolves into a sea of fingerprints.

"I think problem-solving is generally overstressed. The far more important thing is problem creation. If you ask yourself an interesting question, your answer will be personal. It will be interesting just because you put yourself in the position to think differently." Chuck Close

Up Close

Compare *Jasper* and *Fanny/Fingerpainting*

How are they similar? How are the two paintings different? Look closely and list as many similarities and differences as you can find.

• Both are close-up, larger-than-life portrait heads. Fanny faces forward; her neck and the top of her shoulders are visible. The head and neck of Jasper are turned slightly to his left, and his image extends to the edges of the large canvas.

• Both are organized using a grid system. Close varies the placement of the grid. Sometimes it's horizontal-vertical, as with *Fanny's* grid; sometimes it's oriented diagonally, as with *Jasper's*.

• *Fanny* is painted in black and white; *Jasper* is in color.

• An important distinguishing characteristic of Close's portrait heads is how he fills the squares or diamonds of the grid. In *Fanny/Fingerpainting* he used subtly shaded fingerprints to replicate the tones of a black-and-white photograph; the grid lines cannot be seen. His approach to *Jasper* was completely different. Each unit in the grid is composed of multicolored concentric rings, with no two units alike. When viewed up close, each diamond begins to look like a tiny abstract painting. When seen from farther back, however, the colors, shapes, and lines come together to form the image of the artist Jasper Johns.

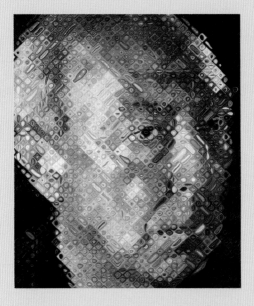

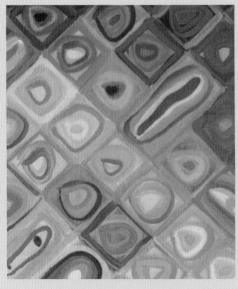

Fanny/Fingerpainting was created before Close became paralyzed. After his spinal artery collapse, Close lost fine motor control in his hands, and he could no longer make fingerpaintings. For *Jasper* and similar paintings, Close attached a paintbrush to his hand and moved his arm to apply the paint onto the canvas.

Chuck Close, *Jasper*, 1997–1998, oil on canvas, National Gallery of Art, Gift of Ian and Annette Cumming

The detail above comes from Jasper's forehead.

"There's a real joy in putting all these little marks together. They may look like hot dogs, but with them I build a painting." Chuck Close

**What choices would
you make when
creating a portrait?**

telling stories

Artists often tell stories through pictures. The artists in this chapter selected stories from religious, mythological, and historical sources, as well as tales from their imaginations. Fra Angelico and Fra Filippo Lippi envisioned an important event from the Bible. Rogier van der Weyden and Raphael painted their own interpretations of the story of Saint George. Peter Paul Rubens chose to show climactic moments from biblical and mythological stories. John Singleton Copley depicted a real-life event with great suspense, while Claude-Joseph Vernet painted imaginary adventures. Augustus Saint-Gaudens and Jacob Lawrence honored heroes of the Civil War era. As you compare the different artists in this chapter, think about what choices artists make when depicting a story and what elements of art contribute to telling it.

Fra Angelico and Fra Filippo
Lippi, *The Adoration of the Magi,*
c. 1440/1460, tempera on panel,
National Gallery of Art, Samuel
H. Kress Collection

1 A Long Journey

As told in the Gospels of the New Testament, the life of
Jesus began with his extraordinary yet humble birth in
Bethlehem. Shepherds and three Magi (wise men from
the East) visited the manger where Jesus was born to
pay their respects. *The Adoration of the Magi* depicts the
moment when the three wise men, bringing gifts of
gold, frankincense, and myhrr, kneel before the infant.
The story of the Magi was particularly popular in

Florence, Italy, in the fifteenth century. The journey of
the three wise men was often depicted in Florentine art
and reenacted in Epiphany processions through the city.

In Renaissance Italy, religious images, from large altarpieces for churches to small paintings for private devotion in homes, were the mainstay of artists' workshops.
At the time, not all common people could read. Stories
from the Bible were reproduced in paintings filled with
symbols that viewers could easily understand.

"When they saw the star, they were overjoyed. On coming to the house, they saw the child with his mother Mary, and they bowed down and worshiped him. Then they opened their treasures and presented him with gifts of gold and of incense and of myrrh." Matthew 2:10 – 11

2 Look Around

The Adoration of the Magi is one of the first examples of a *tondo* (Italian for "round painting"), a popular form for religious paintings in the 1400s. The figures, views of the distant city, and the landscape are all arranged to make the best use of the panel's round shape. A joyful procession of more than a hundred people winds its way down a steep path from the upper right. The line of men and women wraps around the rocky outcropping and enters the city through the arched gateway.

Look closely to find:

Horses, a pheasant, an ox, camels, a dog, and a peacock: Which creature stands out from the crowd? Perched on the roof of the stable, the magnificent peacock was a symbol of immortality.

A bearded man in red: The Magi found their way to Bethlehem by following a bright star. Although the star is not shown in the painting, its presence is indicated by the bearded man on a black horse. He gazes toward the star in the sky and raises his arms in awe.

A pomegranate: Sitting on his mother's lap, the infant Jesus raises his right hand to bless the Magi. In his left hand he holds a pomegranate. Its numerous seeds represent the many people who were brought together by the Christian Church.

Gold: Artists used precious gold leaf to draw attention to the most significant figures in the painting. Jesus, his mother Mary, and Joseph have gold halos. Golden embroidery on their rose, blue, and red robes as well as the glistening aura around their heads help to identify the Magi.

3 Two Artists

More than one artist painted *The Adoration of the Magi*. Although it is unsigned, scholars generally agree that it was created by two master artists in Florence: the Dominican friar Fra Angelico (c. 1395–1455) and the Carmelite monk Fra Filippo Lippi (c. 1406–1469). It is not known, however, how the two artists came to work on the same painting. The *tondo* was in the collection of the Medici, a wealthy family of art patrons in fifteenth-century Florence. Both Fra Angelico and Fra Filippo Lippi regularly created paintings for the powerful Medici family.

One idea is that the older artist, Fra Angelico, designed the composition and began the painting, but for some reason he was unable to complete the project. The painting was then turned over to Lippi to finish. It likely remained in the studio of one artist for several years, and assistants may have worked on it. Art historians who study the unique painting style of each artist believe Lippi painted the Magi, while Fra Angelico was responsible for the face of Mary.

explore more

If It Glitters...
It Might Be Gold!

Gold, one of the most precious metals, has been used by artists around the world. In Renaissance Italy, gold was incorporated into religious paintings to indicate a holy presence or figure and to symbolize the timeless realm of heaven.

Most Italian art created in the thirteenth through sixteenth centuries has a religious theme. It is important to remember that these works were not intended to be hung in a museum—instead, they were made for devotional purposes and decorated churches, private chapels, and homes. When the gold decoration was illuminated by candles, the effect was dazzling.

Painting on Panels

A wooden support, or panel, often of white poplar, lies below most paintings created in Italy in the thirteenth to fifteenth centuries. The panel was covered with size (glue made from animal skin), which kept the paint from soaking into the wood. A bright white gesso (a plaster ground) was applied next. Artists painted with pigments (powdered color) mixed with water and egg, which resulted in bright colors.

For the gold areas of a painting, diluted bole (a reddish-brown clay) was brushed onto the gesso surface. This provided a cushion for the delicate gold leaf (pieces of gold hammered extremely thin). Gold leaf was carefully applied in small sections and then smoothed and polished with a burnisher (a tool with a tip of hard stone). This gave the gold a brilliant, shining surface that could then be tooled (punched with a metal stamp) to create designs and patterns.

Materials and tools used in gilding, including pestle and mortar, knives, bole, and gold leaf (photo: Edward Woodman)

A Step 1: Gesso ground
B Step 2: Bole
C Step 3: Gold leaf, applied in layers
D Step 4: Gold leaf, smoothed with a burnisher

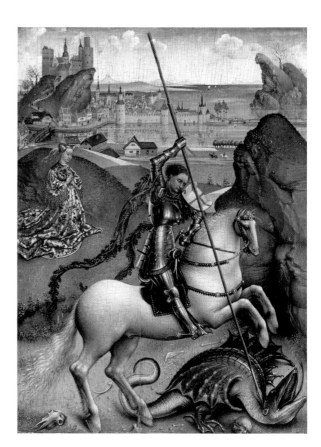

Rogier van der Weyden,
Saint George and the Dragon,
c. 1432/1435, oil on panel,
National Gallery of Art, Ailsa
Mellon Bruce Fund

This painting is only 5⅝ by 4⅛
inches in size!

1 George's Story

The knight in each of these paintings is Saint George, a
Roman soldier who lived during the third century in Asia
Minor (modern-day Turkey). According to a popular
legend from the Middle Ages, Saint George rescued a
princess and her town from a terrible dragon. The best-
known account of this heroic tale was written in *The
Golden Legend,* a medieval best seller from the year 1260.
Its stories from the Bible and tales of the lives of saints
inspired many artists. For early Christians, Saint George
became a symbol of courage, valor, and selflessness.

According to *The Golden Legend,* the citizens of Silene,
a city in Libya, were threatened by a fierce and terrible
dragon. People saved themselves by feeding their sheep
to the hungry monster. When their supply of animals
started to run low, the frightened townspeople realized
they would have to choose a person to sacrifice. Princess
Cleodolinda was the unlucky one selected. Outside the
city walls, she knelt and wept while she waited for the
dragon. Just then, a brave and noble knight passed by
and vowed to save her. George slew the dragon with a
single thrust. The citizens of Silene were so inspired by
this fearless act that they converted to Christianity.

This popular tale of good triumphing over evil was told
to children to inspire them to lead virtuous lives.

2 Masterful Miniatures

Saint George was a favorite subject of artists during the
Middle Ages and the Renaissance. These small paintings
of Saint George, created in different parts of Europe, were
made by two of the leading artists of their times: Rogier
van der Weyden (c. 1399/1400–1464) in northern
Europe, and Raffaello Sanzio, known as Raphael (1483–
1520), in Italy. Despite their diminutive size, each painting is full of incredible details that were meant to be
viewed closely.

Look carefully and compare:

Saint George: Both paintings show the most dramatic
part of the story: when Saint George thrusts his lance
at the ferocious dragon. Notice how each artist painted
the light bouncing off George's brilliant suit of armor.
Examine the expression on his face.

Horse: George rides a white horse in both paintings. Its
movement, with its mouth open and tongue out, adds
to the energy of the scene.

Dragon: Both artists created a frightening version of this mythological creature near its rocky cave.

Princess Cleodolinda: Each artist shows the princess kneeling in prayer and dressed in the current fashion of his own era. Rogier's Cleodolinda wears a rich gold and blue brocade dress and an elaborate headdress. Raphael's princess is dressed in red with a thin golden halo.

Landscape: Each artist set the story in a landscape that resembled his own country. Rogier's painting shows a view over rolling hills toward a walled city surrounded by water and dominated by a castle perched atop a fantastic mountain. Raphael's tall trees and rocky hills direct attention to the towers of a city in the distance.

What other similarities can you find between the two paintings? What are their differences?

3 An Oil-based Revolution

How did these artists create such tiny and highly detailed paintings on wood panels? Both Rogier and Raphael skillfully used oil paints, an invention that changed the history of art.

Early artists had used egg tempera paint. Its powdered pigments—made by grinding colored earth, minerals, and even the shell of certain insects—were blended with egg yolks. Tempera was durable and dried quickly, but it was also thick and could be difficult to mix with other colors. In the early 1400s artists in northern Europe developed a revolutionary way to handle oil paint, which was made by blending pigments with slow-drying linseed or walnut oil. Intricate effects, such as the shine of Saint George's armor, could be achieved using the medium. Artists could build up thin layers of opaque and transparent paint that reflected light, and they could subtly blend wet paint to produce a wide range of new color possibilities.

"George, a native of Cappadocia...once traveled to the city of Silena....Near this town there was a pond as large as a lake where a plague-bearing dragon lurked; and many times the dragon had put the populace to flight when they came out armed against him, for he used to come up to the city walls and poison everyone who came within reach of his breath."

Jacobus de Voragine, *The Golden Legend,* 1260

Dragon Design

Dragons appear in stories from ancient times through to the present day. Sometimes they symbolize evil, as in the story of Saint George, but in China and other countries, dragons are emblems of good luck.

Bestiaries—illustrated books that describe real and legendary animals—were popular references in the Middle Ages.

Artists created these mythological creatures from their imaginations. Sometimes they combined features of several animals. What kinds of animals might have inspired Rogier and Raphael in painting their dragons?

Invent a dragon or imaginary creature

Decide: Will the beast be friendly or dangerous, lucky or evil? Does your creature have any special powers?

Think about: What animals will you combine? Imagine a head of a_____, body of a_____, the claws of a_____, wings of a_____, and tail of a_____.

Sketch out possible ideas and combinations.

Transform your idea into a three-dimensional action figure or puppet by using a combination of art materials (clay, papier-mâché, paint) and found objects (pipe cleaners, egg cartons, cardboard rolls and boxes, paper).

Create a story about your creature. Where did it come from? Where does it live and what does it eat? Who does it meet? Is it the hero or the villain of your story?

Suffrage to Saint George. Playfair Book of Hours. Ms.L.475–1918, fol. 174v. French (Rouen), late 15th c. Victoria and Albert Museum, London, Great Britain. Photo credit: V&A Images, London/Art Resource, NY

Peter Paul Rubens. *Self-portrait with hat* (detail), 1623–1625, oil on wood, Uffizi, Florence, Italy. Photo credit: Scala / Art Resource, NY

1 Painter and Diplomat

Flemish artist Sir Peter Paul Rubens (1577–1640) had a prolific career painting religious and mythological stories, church altarpieces, palace decorations, royal portraits, and intimate family scenes. Not only was he one of the most acclaimed painters of his time, but he was also a scholar, teacher, linguist (he knew seven languages), collector of antiquities, and diplomat.

Rubens traveled from his home in Antwerp to study in Italy from 1600 to 1609. There he was inspired by classical sculpture, the paintings of Raphael and Michelangelo, and Caravaggio's dramatic works that contrast light and shadow. Rubens returned to Antwerp, where his artistic talents were quickly recognized and his popularity grew. Rubens was appointed court painter to Archduke Albert and his wife, Isabella. He established a large workshop with apprentices and assistants to help him complete his numerous commissions.

Paralleling Rubens' unrivaled artistic career was his increased involvement in politics and diplomatic missions. While traveling for royal commissions, Rubens served as a cultural envoy and helped negotiate treaties. Among his many noble patrons was King Charles I of England, who knighted Rubens for his work as a peace mediator between Spain and England.

Daniel in the Lions' Den, once owned by Charles I, shows how Rubens masterfully combined realism and theatricality to produce a strong emotional impact.

2 Daniel's Dramatic Story

The story of the Hebrew prophet Daniel comes from the Old Testament. Daniel aroused the envy of the other royal ministers when he became the chief counselor to the Persian king Darius. These jealous men tricked the king into ordering Daniel's death. They passed a law that said people could pray only to the king and not to any god. When it was discovered that Daniel kept praying to God as he always had, he was condemned to spend the night in the den of ferocious, hungry lions. In the morning, King Darius rushed out to see what had happened. Miraculously, Daniel had survived the night unharmed!

Rubens shows the scene inside the lions' den. Surrounded by the dangerous beasts, Daniel prays and looks toward heaven with gratitude. Bones on the ground are a grim reminder of what could have happened. Daniel became a symbol of justice, and his story demonstrated the importance of faith.

"Daniel among many lions, taken from life. Original, entirely by my hand." **Peter Paul Rubens**

3 Taken from Life

Snarling, pacing, sleeping, yawning, and staring: the ten lions in this painting look frightening and amazingly real. How did Rubens manage to paint these animals in such a lifelike way? He studied lions in the royal menagerie of Brussels and in the zoo of Ghent. He made detailed drawings of the animals' movements, expressions, and behaviors.

His use of light, color, space, and scale emphasizes the physical and emotional drama of the scene. By painting the lions nearly life-size, Rubens makes it feel as if we are in the den with Daniel. Morning light streams into the dark cave through an opening, illuminating Daniel's gestures, sculpted muscles, and anguished expression. His red and white robes stand out against the brown tones of the lions' den. Rubens even added blood red paint around the mouths of some lions for a terrifying effect!

above: Peter Paul Rubens, *Daniel in the Lions' Den*, c. 1614/1616, oil on canvas, National Gallery of Art, Ailsa Mellon Bruce Fund

This painting is over 7 by 10 feet in size!

right: Peter Paul Rubens, *Lion*, c. 1612–1613, black chalk, heightened with white, yellow chalk in the background, National Gallery of Art, Ailsa Mellon Bruce Fund

A stone was brought and placed over the mouth of the den.... At the first light of dawn, the king got up and hurried to the lions' den. When he came near the den, he called to Daniel in an anguished voice.... Daniel answered, "May the King live forever! My God sent his angel, and he shut the mouths of the lions. They have not hurt me." **Daniel 6:17 – 22**

Myth in Motion

The Fall of Phaeton by Rubens is another example of the artist's exceptional ability for dramatic storytelling. The myth, recounted by the Roman poet Ovid, describes Phaeton's doomed journey across the sky.

The Tragedy of Phaeton

According to classical mythology, the Roman god Phoebus Apollo (called Helios by the Greeks) drove the chariot of the sun across the sky each day, thus giving the earth its hours and seasons. His son, Phaeton, was a mortal. When the boy was teased because he claimed his father was a god, Phaeton asked Phoebus Apollo to prove he was his parent. In response, Phoebus Apollo promised Phaeton anything he wanted. Phaeton impulsively demanded to drive his father's chariot for one day. Although Phoebus Apollo knew the boy couldn't control the horses, he felt he could not deny his son's request and handed over the reins.

The chariot ran wild, scorching everything in its path with the sun's heat. To prevent the earth's destruction, Jupiter, the king of the gods, intervened. He hurled a thunderbolt at the chariot and sent it in a fiery plunge to earth.

Peter Paul Rubens, *The Fall of Phaeton*, c. 1604/1605, probably reworked c. 1606/1608, oil on canvas, National Gallery of Art, Patrons' Permanent Fund

Rubens' Dramatic Style

Rubens created this painting while he was studying in Italy. An inventive artist, he chose to depict the story at the height of its action, when the thunderbolt streaks in from the right and Phaeton plummets to the earth. The artist included figures with butterfly wings to symbolize the hours and the seasons; they gesture in horror as the pattern of night and day is disrupted. He also conveys the chaos that occurred when Phaeton lost control of the chariot. Everything in his dynamic composition is in motion—figures twist and tumble, and horses rear. The strong contrast between light and dark further intensifies the drama.

Rubens often chose to show the climax, or most dramatic moment, of a story.

Choose a story that interests you and make a drawing showing the most climatic moment.

With a splitting crack of thunder
  he lifted a bolt,
Poised it by his ear,
Then drove the barbed flash point-blank
  into Phaeton.
The explosion
Snuffed the ball of flame
As it blew the chariot to fragments. Phaeton
Went spinning out of his life.

The crazed horses scattered.
They tore free, with scraps of the yoke,
Trailing their broken reins.
The wreckage fell through space,
Shattered wheels gyrating apart,
Shards of the car, the stripped axle,
Bits of harness—all in slow motion
Sprinkled through emptiness.

Phaeton, hair ablaze,
A fiery speck, lengthening a vapour trail,
Plunged toward earth
Like a star
Falling and burning out on a clear night.

—excerpt from Ted Hughes' *Tales from Ovid*

"The Monster was already too near him for the youth to be timely apprized of his danger; and the sailors had the afflicting sight of seeing him seized and precipitated down the flood with his voracious assailant, before they could put off to attempt his deliverance. They however hastened towards the place...." **From the inscription on the painting's original frame**

John Singleton Copley, *Watson and the Shark*, 1778, oil on canvas, National Gallery of Art, Ferdinand Lammot Belin Fund

This painting was a huge success and launched Copley's career in England. The artist painted a full-scale replica for himself. It is now in the Museum of Fine Arts, Boston.

Danger!

Watson and the Shark depicts a real event that took place in the harbor at Havana, Cuba, in 1749. Brook Watson was a fourteen-year-old orphan who worked on a trading ship. One day he went swimming in the warm waters of the harbor and was attacked by a shark. As his shipmates rushed to his rescue, the shark circled around again, pulling Watson underwater and biting off his right foot.

John Singleton Copley, *The Copley Family*, 1776/1777, oil on canvas, National Gallery of Art, Andrew W. Mellon Fund

2 Heroism!

Thanks to the sailors' quick actions, Watson lived to tell his story. It took him three months to recover. His leg was amputated below the knee, and he was fitted with a wooden leg that he wore for the rest of his long life. He later moved to England, where he became a successful politician and businessman. Almost thirty years after the attack, Watson hired artist John Singleton Copley (1738–1815) to record his amazing rescue story for history. Years later, he gave the painting to a boys' school, hoping his bravery might inspire others to overcome life's challenges. It also served as a lesson about the risks of foolish behavior.

3 Suspense!

One of the most talented artists in colonial America, Copley moved from Boston in 1775, on the eve of the American Revolution, and settled with his family in London, England. He had never been to Cuba. To create an accurate background view of the harbor's buildings and ships, he studied maps and prints of Havana. Copley had never seen a tiger shark either. Notice the shark's oddly shaped nostrils, strange lips, and ear. It might not be accurate, but it's still a scary-looking shark!

Copley focused on the moment right before Watson was rescued. The boy's fate is still uncertain. He struggles in the water as the terrifying shark comes back, opening its powerful jaws to attack once more. Watson's mouth and eyes are wide open in fear. The shark is just inches away. He reaches his hand up toward his rescuers. Will he make it?

Copley packed nine men into the small rescue boat. Four sailors pull their oars to maneuver closer to Watson. Two young seamen lean over the gunwale, straining to reach the frightened boy, while their bald-headed mate grabs onto a shirt. One standing sailor throws out a rope, and another thrusts his harpoon at the shark.

Look closely at the faces and gestures of the sailors
How do you think each one feels? The range of expressions heightens the tension and reality of the moment.

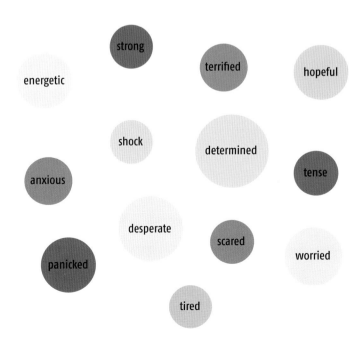

Claude-Joseph Vernet

Action-Adventure-Imagination

The painting *Watson and the Shark* recounts a real-life event, but French artist Claude-Joseph Vernet (1714–1789), like many artists, made up a dramatic scene. This vivid painting of a shipwreck is a lot like an action-adventure movie. It's an imaginary story, created to thrill, frighten, and delight viewers. Think about creating a sound track to go along with this picture. What sounds would enhance the horror of this tragic shipwreck?

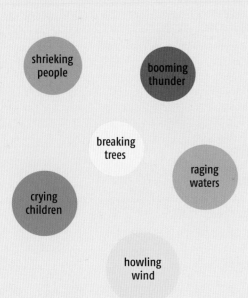

shrieking people

booming thunder

breaking trees

raging waters

crying children

howling wind

Vernet specialized in painting stormy seascapes. What artistic choices add to the drama of the scene? Illuminated by a yellow zigzag of lightning, the dark sky is painted a menacing gray with touches of purples and blues. The foamy waves of the green sea crash against the rocky shore. The ship's flag whips in the howling wind, its sails torn to shreds, its mast tilting at a dangerous angle. A tree on the cliff has been splintered. Only the castle in the distance stands strong. Everyone works frantically to secure the ship, save its supplies, and rescue the survivors. Their poses express fear, exhaustion, and relief. Through this physical and emotional struggle, Vernet shows the overwhelming power of nature. What do you think will happen next? Will the ship in the distance avoid the storm, or will it suffer the same fate?

Some paintings are meant to make you feel happy or peaceful, while others are designed to worry or scare you. Vernet created paintings that did both. Although the shipwreck is imaginary, he described the horrible experience in a way that stirs emotions.

Suspenseful Stories

Create your own scary adventure inspired by the following prompts:

It was a dark and stormy night...

Suddenly the lights went out and...

It started out small but then...

The creaking door opened ever so slowly...

Or start your own!

Claude-Joseph Vernet, *The Shipwreck*, 1772, oil on canvas, National Gallery of Art, Patrons' Permanent Fund and Chester Dale Fund

The most famous landscape and maritime painter in eighteenth-century France, Vernet was admired for his ability to combine the spectacular effects of weather with detailed, lively figures.

Augustus Saint-Gaudens, *Memorial to Robert Gould Shaw and the Massachusetts 54th Regiment*, 1900, patinated plaster, on loan from U.S. Department of the Interior, National Park Service, Saint-Gaudens National Historic Site, Cornish, New Hampshire

1 In Procession

This life-size sculpture commemorates members of the Massachusetts 54th Regiment, one of the first African American units to serve in the Civil War. A thousand African American men from across the country volunteered to join this regiment and fight for the Union. The American Civil War, which raged from 1861 to 1865, was a conflict between the North (Union) and South (Confederacy) of the United States. One of the central issues over which the two sides fought was slavery.

Colonel Robert Gould Shaw, the leader of the 54th Regiment, rides gallantly on horseback alongside his men. He was a young white man from a family in Boston that strongly opposed slavery.

This powerful sculpture shows Colonel Shaw and his regiment as they marched off on May 28, 1863, to fight in the Civil War. A large crowd gathered in downtown Boston to send them off. Among the black soldiers marching that day were Frederick Douglass's two sons, Lewis and Charles; James Caldwell, the grandson of Sojourner Truth; and William Caleney, who would become the first African American to be awarded the Congressional Medal of Honor.

Colonel Robert G. Shaw / Whipple (detail), 96 Washington Street, Boston. Library of Congress Prints and Photographs Division, Washington, DC

2 In Memory

In July 1863, the 54th Regiment led an attack against Fort Wagner, a fortress protecting the harbor of Charleston, South Carolina, deep in Confederate territory. Almost half of the soldiers who stormed the fort were killed, captured, or later died of their wounds, including Colonel Shaw.

The bravery and determination of the 54th Regiment earned great respect for black soldiers and inspired widespread enlistment of African Americans into the Union forces. By the end of the Civil War, nearly 180,000 black soldiers had fought for the Union. Their contributions and sacrifices, President Abraham Lincoln later said, gave the Union the advantage to win. In 1865 the South surrendered, and the United States remained one nation.

Right in the van,
On the red rampart's slippery swell,
With heart that beat a charge, he fell
Forward, as fits a man;
But the high soul burns on to light men's feet
Where death for noble ends makes dying sweet.
"Memoriam Positum," John Russell Lowell, 1863,
inscribed on the memorial

3 In Relief

A relief is a type of sculpture that is raised from a flat surface rather than being sculpted "in the round." Coins and medals are examples of low relief, with images on them raised slightly from the surface. The Shaw Memorial was done in high relief, with the images projecting far from the surface. You can almost see all the way around Colonel Shaw and his horse.

The sculptor Augustus Saint-Gaudens (1848–1907) used a photograph of Colonel Shaw to show his facial features and uniform accurately. He wanted the monument to be as realistic as possible, and he even brought a horse into his studio to work from a live model.

Each soldier is unique. Some of the soldiers in the 54th Regiment were as young as sixteen years old. Others were fathers enlisting with their sons. To give each man a sense of individuality, Saint-Gaudens hired several African Americans to pose for him.

How might these men have felt about fighting in the Civil War?

scared · dedicated · proud · serious · hopeful · determined

Camp Scene Evening Amusements (Annapolis)

Bogues Banks (Sunset)

8th Ct marching in the City Washington Septbr 5th 1862.

Civil War Sketchbook: A Soldier's Perspective

During the Civil War, many soldiers kept journals and sketchbooks as a way to record their memories of friends, daily life, new places, and military actions. These important documents of history not only help us understand what their experiences were like, but they also provide significant details about the time.

Civil War soldier Corporal J. E. Shadek, a member of Company A of the 8th Connecticut Volunteers, filled a small journal with ninety-three drawings—sketches of battlefields, encampments, soldiers' daily activities, and other events during his years as a soldier in the Union Army's Burnside Expedition in 1861 and 1862.

Keep a visual journal

Try to carry a sketchbook with you one day a week and stop to record a person, place, activity, or event that you observe—in your home, neighborhood, school, or on a trip. It might be an everyday occurrence or something unique that you notice. It might be a quick five-minute sketch or a longer drawing. Write the date at the bottom of each sketch. If you wish, paste photographs into the sketchbook alongside your drawings. At the end of twelve months, you'll have a visual diary recording your memories of the year.

J. E. Shadek, *J. E. Shadek Sketchbook*, 1861/1862, bound volume with 93 drawings in mixed media on wove paper, National Gallery of Art, Gift of Mrs. Halleck Lefferts

top: Soldiers entertaining themselves around an evening campfire, Annapolis, Maryland 1861

middle: Sunset painted while camped at Bogues Banks, North Carolina

bottom: Troops marching in Washington, DC, September 5, 1862

1 Painter and Storyteller

Jacob Lawrence (1917–2000) was inspired to paint the everyday life he saw around him as well as to tell epic stories of American history.

Born in Atlantic City, New Jersey, Lawrence and his family moved to Harlem in New York City in 1930, when he was thirteen years old. Despite the poverty of the Great Depression, African American intellectual and artistic life was flourishing in Harlem, and Lawrence became interested in the arts while he was still a teenager. He began painting in after-school art classes at the Harlem Art Workshops, where he learned about the styles of Vincent van Gogh, Henri Matisse, and African art. Charles Alston, Augusta Savage, and other prominent artists in the community who were impressed by his talent and creative vision encouraged Lawrence to pursue art as a career. He enjoyed visiting the Metropolitan Museum of Art, where he was particularly drawn to Renaissance art and to scenes painted by Mexican muralist Diego Rivera. By combining these influences, Lawrence developed a style that was both figural and abstract.

Interested in the history, accomplishments, and struggles of black people, Lawrence often painted in series as a way to tell a story. He gained fame for his powerful narratives of the lives of such historic figures as Toussaint L'Ouverture, Harriet Tubman, Frederick Douglass, and John Brown. He described the journey of those who made the great African American migration from the rural South to cities in the North in search of a better life, while his later works document events during World War II and the Civil Rights Movement. The paintings of Jacob Lawrence express his lifelong concern for human dignity and freedom, and his own social consciousness.

2 Honoring Harriet Tubman

Born a slave on the Eastern Shore of Maryland, Harriet Tubman escaped to freedom and ultimately made her way to Philadelphia, Pennsylvania. During the 1850s and 1860s, she courageously returned to the South nineteen times, helping more than three hundred slaves escape to freedom in Canada.

Traveling under the cover of night, Tubman used the North Star as a guide and followed the Underground Railroad, a network of people that helped slaves escape to freedom. By day, the slaves hid secretly in houses along the route. Risking her life to liberate others, Tubman demonstrated strength, courage, tenacity, and self-sacrifice. She worked as a nurse during the Civil War and later as an advocate for the rights of African Americans and women.

In 1939 and 1940 Lawrence created a series of thirty-one panels that describe moments in Tubman's life. He revisited the subject in 1967, when he wrote and illustrated the children's book *Harriet and the Promised Land* and created independent paintings such as *Daybreak—A Time to Rest*.

"The struggle of the American people is a really beautiful thing. It's a symbol of what can be achieved." Jacob Lawrence

"When the subjects are strong, I believe simplicity is the best way of treating them." **Jacob Lawrence**

3 Simplified Color and Form

In *Daybreak — A Time to Rest,* Lawrence conveys Harriet Tubman's bravery and her role as a protector with his dramatic style of vivid colors, flattened shapes, and simplified forms.

Near the center of the composition Tubman's face turns upward to the sky, and her body is surrounded by purple and pink cloaks. The night sky came to symbolize Tubman, as Frederick Douglass later described in a letter he wrote to her: "The midnight sky and the silent stars have been the witnesses of your devotion to freedom and of your heroism." Lying on the hard ground, she holds a rifle at the ready for protection. The exaggerated perspective, which makes her feet look enormous, emphasizes the arduous journeys she made. Forming a crescent above Tubman's head, a man, woman, and baby huddle together closely, resting. Three insects — a walking stick, beetle, and ant — crawl on the large green leaves in the foreground and signal activity at daybreak.

"The Human subject is the most important thing. My work is abstract in the sense of having been designed and composed, but it is not abstract in the sense of having no human content.... I want to communicate. I want the idea to strike right away." **Jacob Lawrence**

far left: Jacob Lawrence (detail), c. 1950s (photo: Sid Bernstein), Jacob Lawrence and Gwendolyn Knight papers, Archives of American Art, Smithsonian Institution

left: Portrait of Harriet Tubman (detail), 1880. Courtesy of the Library of Congress Prints and Photographs Division, Washington, DC

above: Jacob Lawrence, *Daybreak — A Time to Rest,* 1967, tempera on hardboard, National Gallery of Art, Anonymous Gift

"I became so excited then by all the new visual forms I found in Nigeria — unusual color combinations, textures, shapes, and the dramatic effect of light — that I felt an overwhelming desire to come back as soon as possible to steep myself in Nigerian culture so that my paintings, if I'm fortunate, might show the influence of the great African artistic tradition." Jacob Lawrence

Inspired by Nigeria

Lawrence traveled to Nigeria in 1962 on an invitation to teach and exhibit his work. Two years later he returned for an eight-month stay and painted aspects of everyday life, including *Street to Mbari*.

Here, he captures the hustle and bustle of a busy outdoor market. Shops and vendors line the street far into the distance. People young and old buy and sell produce and rolls of boldly patterned fabrics, while women balance wares on their heads. It is easy to imagine the sounds of this crowded market — people chatting, babies crying, goats bleating, chickens squawking, flies buzzing, carts rolling — and to feel the energy of the scene.

Throughout his career, Lawrence preferred to paint with vivid opaque water-based paints (tempera or gouache) on board or paper. He carefully planned his composition by making a line drawing first, and then he filled in each area, one color at a time. The thin white lines that define and give character to eyes, ears, nostrils, fingernails, and toenails are white paper left unpainted. Repeating colors and shapes emphasize the energy and movement of the scene. The colors of the patterned fabrics and clothing mirror the colors on the ground and in the sky. Stripes of brown-colored paint, giving the appearance of corrugated iron roofs, create a visual rhythm across the top of the painting and lead the eye into the distance.

Look

Observe the colors, shapes, and lines in detail.

Colors: What colors do you see? Describe them.

Shapes: What kinds of shapes do you see? Describe them.

Lines: What kinds of lines do you see? Describe them.

Jacob Lawrence, *Street to Mbari*, 1964, tempera over graphite on wove paper, National Gallery of Art, Gift of Mr. and Mrs. James T. Dyke

Discuss

Choose a color, shape, or line that you noticed. Consider these questions:

• How does it contribute to the mood of the painting?

• How does it contribute to the way the scene looks?

• How does it contribute to a story the artwork might tell?

Reflect

What new ideas do you have about the artwork?

How might you tell
a story without words?

chapter five

observing everyday life

Food, friends and families, neighborhoods, work and leisure activities – these are the staples of everyday life. This chapter features artists who have taken notice of the people and objects that make up their world. Jan Steen and Hendrick Avercamp recorded the sights and sounds of the seventeenth-century Dutch Republic, while still-life paintings by Osias Beert the Elder, Willem Claesz Heda, and Jan Davidsz de Heem convey the prosperity of their time. Édouard Manet painted people whose very existence was changed by the urban growth of Paris. Mary Cassatt became well known for her paintings of mothers and children in natural poses. Winslow Homer turned his attention to people at work and play, while Wayne Thiebaud pays tribute to the traditions of American life by painting some familiar and delicious treats. As you consider the diverse artists in this chapter, think about the many ways everyday life inspires art.

1 Painter and Storyteller

Dutch artist Jan Steen (1625/1626–1679) painted stories of daily life, showing merry scenes of family gatherings, rowdy parties, and misbehaving people. His lively, detailed images were meant to be entertaining, but they also sent messages about how *not* to behave. Viewers in the seventeenth century would have laughed at Steen's humor and nodded in agreement with his moralizing stories. Paintings that capture everyday life, called genre scenes, were among the most popular in Dutch art at that time.

These paintings were designed to delight the senses. Imagine you could step into this festive scene. What might you hear? Taste? Smell? Feel? See?

above: Jan Steen, *Self-Portrait*
(detail), c. 1670, oil on canvas,
Rijksmuseum, Amsterdam

right: Jan Steen, *The Dancing
Couple*, 1663, oil on canvas,
National Gallery of Art, Widener
Collection

2 Join the Party!

Under the vine-covered trellis at this country inn people are talking, laughing, flirting, and dancing. What is the occasion? Look behind the dancing man. The tents in the background are probably part of a village festival called a *kermis* in Dutch. People traveled from near and far to meet up with friends, share news, shop, or marvel at goods for sale at a *kermis*. Children also had fun—like the boy on the right, blowing a bubble. Can you spot the girl playing with a pinwheel? Pinwheels could be purchased at fairs, which was the closest thing to a toy store most seventeenth-century children would ever experience. On the left, a baby

3 What a Mess!

No one in this crowd seems concerned about the mess on the floor. Broken eggs, spilled flowers, and the bubbles blown by the boy all symbolize the fragility of life. Steen often included such details to remind viewers not to be too silly or wild and to remember what is important in life. The artist was well known for his paintings of disorder and disarray. Even today in Holland, a messy home is sometimes called a "Jan Steen household."

stands on her mother's lap, holding a hammer toy. The little men raise and lower their hammers in harmony when she pulls on the ends of the toy.

In this painting Steen celebrates a harmonious life, with people of all ages and from different social classes having a good time together. To highlight their diverse relationships, the artist arranged many of the figures in pairs. Find a couple dancing, a pair of musicians playing, and two children talking together. Steen even included himself with his wife, Margriet van Goyen. He's the man with long black hair seated at the table and tickling the chin of the woman next to him.

Winter Wonders

Hendrick Avercamp (1585–1634) was one of the first Dutch artists to specialize in depicting the landscape and daily activities during winter. After training as an artist in Amsterdam, he became a very successful painter in his hometown of Kampen. Family records indicate Avercamp was deaf throughout his life.

Canals and rivers in the Netherlands froze during the winter months. For nearly three hundred years, from about 1550 to 1850, a phenomenon known as the Little Ice Age produced unusually harsh, long winters in Europe. Ice fishing, riding sleighs, ice skating, and the game of *kolf* were some of the popular outdoor activities people enjoyed in the seventeenth century.

In *A Scene on the Ice,* Avercamp shows a variety of people—men and women, young and old, rich and poor—working and playing on a frozen river. His keen eye for detail provides a glimpse into everyday life in the Netherlands on a winter day.

On this wintry day, people dress for the cold by putting on gloves and boots. Gentlemen keep warm by wearing top hats or fur caps and wool capes, while ladies are clad in hooded cloaks and hand muffs. Roofs covered with snow and smoke rising from chimneys further suggest the chilly climate.

Look closely to find:

- a couple ice skating

- fishermen trekking across the ice with their poles

- a group of people loading a sledge with supplies (Because boats were frozen into the ice, goods had to be transported across the river with sledges—large sleds that people could push or horses could pull.)

- a man who took off his gloves to fasten his skates

- two boys playing *kolf* (*Kolf,* which means "club" in Dutch, is a cross between ice hockey and golf. The sport originated in the thirteenth century, but it became very popular in the seventeenth century. Players tried to hit a target, such as a pole in the ice, with as few strokes as possible. *Kolf* was also played on land, but the large expanses of ice in winter made an ideal playing field.)

- well-dressed ladies in an elegant horse-drawn sleigh trimmed with bells (The horse's head is adorned with plumes made of wool and feathers, and its horseshoes are spiked for traction on the slippery ice.)

Imagine: If you could step into this wintry scene, what might you hear? Smell? Feel? See? What activity would you choose to do?

Hendrick Avercamp, *A Scene on the Ice,* c. 1625, oil on panel, National Gallery of Art, Ailsa Mellon Bruce Fund

Osias Beert the Elder, *Dishes with Oysters, Fruit, and Wine,* c. 1620/1625, oil on panel, National Gallery of Art, Patrons' Permanent Fund

1 Hungry for New Foods

In Holland four hundred years ago, daily meals consisted of bread and butter, cheese, fruit, fish, and stews of meats and vegetables. With expanding international trade in the seventeenth century, a wider variety of foods became available. Dutch ships traveled around the world in search of luxury items: salt from France and Portugal; grains from Poland and Prussia; raisins, dates, figs, nuts, and olives from the Mediterranean; sugar from the Caribbean and Brazil; and pepper, nutmeg, cloves, cinnamon, and other spices from Indonesia. Paintings of these rare and expensive delicacies were especially popular.

2 A Feast for the Eyes

Paintings of elaborate arrangements of exotic foods were created to delight the senses of sight, smell, touch, and taste. Artists recorded with great detail the textures of objects—the rough peel of a lemon, the translucence of glass, the softness of a linen tablecloth. Still-life paintings were valued for their subject matter as well as for the artist's skill. By carefully observing the natural world, artists strove to achieve an astonishing degree of illusion.

3 Tempting Treats

Dishes with Oysters, Fruit, and Wine by Osias Beert the Elder (c. 1580–1624) presents elegant sweets meticulously arranged on a tabletop in fine bowls and platters for a special occasion.

Beert invites you to select from:

freshly shucked oysters

candied cinnamon bark and candied almonds

quince jelly (stored in round wooden boxes)

pastries

dried raisins, figs, and chestnuts

4 Lavish Banquets

Willem Claesz Heda (1593/1594–1680) specialized in banquet scenes. Set in a dining room owned by a wealthy merchant, Heda's *Banquet Piece with Mince Pie* presents the remains of a sumptuous banquet served on expensive dishes made of gold, pewter, and ivory.

Clues that this meal is over include:

tipped goblets

a snuffed-out candle

a rumpled tablecloth

half-eaten food

platters resting at the edge of the table

The main course was mince pie. Made of rich meat flavored with fruit, currants, raisins, and spices, it was a special dish reserved for holidays and feasts. Slices of fresh lemon add flavor.

Willem Claesz Heda, *Banquet Piece with Mince Pie,* **1635, oil on canvas, National Gallery of Art, Patrons' Permanent Fund**

While depicting beauty and abundance, symbols of living well, these paintings also conveyed moral and religious messages. They were intended to remind viewers of the need for moderation and the brevity of life.

A Fragrant Bounty

Jan Davidsz de Heem (1606–1683/1684) was known for his ability to create paintings of objects that look amazingly real. With his versatile technique, he could paint a wide range of textures—from a soft blossom and a drop of water to a hard table top—in a convincing manner. Despite this realistic depiction, the arrangement of flowers could not have really existed: the vase holds more than twenty kinds of plants, some of which grow at different times of the year. Although De Heem relies on the exact observation of nature, his painting emphasizes the importance of the artist's imagination. He harmoniously arranged a bouquet that will be in bloom forever.

Discover:

• long stalks of wheat

• a caterpillar wiggling along the stem of a big, white poppy

• three butterflies

• a black-and-white honeybee perched atop a red and white poppy

• peas in their pods

• pink roses

• a spider lowering itself to the marble shelf, where a small lizard hungrily waits for it

• two snails

• tiny ants

• a window reflected in the glass vase

• red and white striped tulips

Dutch gardeners were experts in botany, the science of plants. They studied new kinds of flowers that were imported by merchants and brought back by traders traveling the globe. Tulips, which came to the Netherlands from Turkey in the late sixteenth century, were especially popular. Painters depicted colorful tulips and other rare and expensive flowers in their works, making them available for others to study and enjoy, even in the middle of the cold winter.

Jan Davidsz de Heem, *Vase of Flowers*, c. 1660, oil on canvas, National Gallery of Art, Andrew W. Mellon Fund

1 Painter of Modern Life

A native of Paris, Édouard Manet (1832–1883) believed art should be about modern life and embraced the role of social commentator.

Born into a wealthy family, Manet was good-looking, charming, and cosmopolitan, and he was friends with many avant-garde artists and writers. While he admired paintings by the great artists of the past that he saw in the Louvre, Manet did not paint traditional subjects from history, mythology, or religion. Instead, he turned to the world around him: the grand boulevards, fashionable cafés, busy racetracks, and people and activities in his own neighborhood.

Manet's bold style of painting was as revolutionary as his subjects. He used broad, unblended patches of color that seemed to flatten the space in his paintings. When *The Railway* was exhibited in 1874, reviewers criticized its unfinished appearance, unusual composition, and the absence of the rail station itself. These qualities, for which Manet is now admired, were neither understood nor appreciated by audiences accustomed to smoothly finished and detailed paintings in which the story was easily perceived. Manet's art, however, inspired a whole generation of younger painters, including Claude Monet, Edgar Degas, and Auguste Renoir, who later became known as the impressionists.

Henri Fantin-Latour, *Édouard Manet* (detail), 1867, oil on canvas, Stickney Fund, 1905.207, The Art Institute of Chicago. Photography © The Art Institute of Chicago

2 Changing Times

During Manet's lifetime, the urban landscape of Paris changed dramatically. Napoleon III appointed Baron Georges Haussmann to rebuild and modernize the capital city of France. Haussmann transformed Paris by creating new water and sewer systems, railway stations, and bridges. He replaced the city's old, narrow, and winding streets with wide, straight boulevards. The railroad, in particular, became a symbol of progress and modernization. Steam locomotives carried passengers farther and quicker than ever before, and they transported workers from the countryside to labor in new industries.

Édouard Manet, *The Railway*, 1873, oil on canvas, National Gallery of Art, Gift of Horace Havemeyer in memory of his mother, Louisine W. Havemeyer

The woman is Victorine Meurent, Manet's favorite model in the 1860s. The child is the daughter of a fellow artist who allowed Manet to use his garden to paint *The Railway*.

> "You must be of your time and paint what you see."
> **Édouard Manet**

3 The Railway

Manet's *The Railway* shows two fashionably dressed people in the bustling city of Paris. A seated woman pauses from her reading and looks directly toward us. A small puppy naps in her lap, nestled between a folded fan and her open book. A young girl grasps the black iron railing and gazes into the distance. Clouds of steam from a passing train hide the train tracks and billow over a signalman's hut.

Wonder: Manet introduces many questions in this painting, but he provides few answers. How are these figures related? Are they mother and daughter, two sisters, or a nanny with a child? Are they waiting for a train to arrive? Have they just seen someone depart? Or are they taking a break during a long walk?

The artist makes the composition visually interesting by including contrasts and opposites.

The woman wears a long, deep blue dress with white trim, while the young girl wears a short, white dress trimmed with a big blue bow.

The girl's hair is tied up with a thin, black ribbon. The woman's long hair is down, fanning over her shoulders. She wears a thin black ribbon around her neck.

The woman is seated; the girl is standing.

The woman looks at us, while the girl looks away, with her back toward us. What might have caught the young girl's attention? What is the woman looking at?

Like many artists of his time, Manet was fascinated by this transformation, and he painted scenes of the modernized city. *The Railway* is set outside of the Gare Saint-Lazare, the largest and busiest train station in Paris. The white stone pillar and section of iron grillwork in the background are part of the newly built Pont de l'Europe, a massive iron bridge that connected six large avenues over the railroad tracks. By calling the work *The Railway*, Manet emphasizes the importance of the train, even while steam obscures the locomotive itself.

The neighborhood of the Gare Saint-Lazare was part of Manet's daily life. He moved into a studio close to the station in 1872. In fact, the door and window of his studio are visible in the background to the left.

"The life of our city is rich in poetic and marvelous subjects."
Charles Baudelaire, 1846

Édouard Manet, *The Old Musician*, 1862, oil on canvas, National Gallery of Art, Chester Dale Collection

Under the direction of Baron Haussmann, old neighborhoods in Paris were torn down to make way for wide boulevards, bigger buildings, and new bridges. In his paintings, Manet chronicled the changes taking place, including the busy cafes, crowded train stations, and large parks. In *The Old Musician*, he shows the less-glamorous side of modern life.

Jean Lagrène, age 66, Bohemian born at Repiwiller, albumin print (photo: Jacques-Philippe Potteau), Musée du quai Branly/Scala/Art Resource, NY

Manet's Urban Subjects

In 1861 Manet moved to a new studio in the district of Batignolles nearby an area known as Petit Pologne, which was home to the poor who were being uprooted and displaced by urban renewal. Manet presents characters from his neighborhood. Most are real individuals. The seated violinist was Jean Lagrène, the leader of a local gypsy band who earned his living as an organ grinder and artist's model. The man wearing a top hat was a rag picker named Colardet. The dark-haired street urchin was Alexandre, while the blond one was Léon, a boy who worked for Manet. The old man dressed in fur at the painting's edge was called Guéroult.

By painting these people on a monumental scale—the large canvas is six feet by eight feet in size—Manet was making a statement about those who lived on the margins of society in Paris. Although he presents them with a certain sense of detachment, Manet was likely sympathetic to their poverty and homelessness, and he gives them the dignity that was probably denied them in real life.

Mary Cassatt (detail), 1914. Courtesy of Frederick Sweet's research materials on Mary Cassatt and James A. McNeill Whistler, 1872–1975, Archives of American Art, Smithsonian Institution

1 An American in Paris

Mary Stevenson Cassatt (1844–1926) is best known for her paintings of mothers and children. She became a successful professional artist at a time when it was very difficult for a woman to do so.

Cassatt was born into an affluent family in Pennsylvania. Her parents believed it was important for women to receive an education, so she attended school and traveled in Europe during her childhood. This early exposure to the art and culture of Europe greatly influenced the young girl.

After studying art in Philadelphia, Cassatt wanted to return on her own to Paris, then the center of the modern art world. She struggled to convince her parents, since this was a highly unusual undertaking for a young woman. They eventually agreed. Once in Paris, Cassatt studied art on her own, visiting museums across Europe and training in the studios of established artists. (The main art school in Paris, the École des Beaux-Arts, did not accept female students at that time.)

2 Impressionist Connection

Early in her career, Cassatt experimented with different styles of painting, and she soon began to paint scenes of modern life in Paris—but she was not a bohemian artist. Comfortable in her own social milieu, she depicted her family, friends, and their children. Ladies seated in the theater, women reading or drinking tea in their homes or gardens, mothers giving their babies a bath, and children playing were parts of her everyday world.

Cassatt's ability to capture a moment in time drew the attention of French artist Edgar Degas, who invited the artist to exhibit her work with the impressionists

in 1879. The painters known as the impressionists depicted fleeting moments in nature and human life, and they experimented with bright colors, loose brush-strokes, and innovative viewpoints. These techniques reflected a dynamic new approach to painting.

Cassatt's artistic talent, understanding of French language and culture, and independent thinking earned her the respect of this exceptional group of artists, which included Claude Monet, Auguste Renoir, Camille Pissarro, and Alfred Sisley. Among the impressionists, she was one of three women—and the only American.

3 Cassatt's Children

Cassatt transformed ordinary subjects with her fresh vision. Her ability to depict children fully absorbed in their own worlds is evident in *The Boating Party, Children Playing on the Beach,* and *Little Girl in a Blue Armchair.* These paintings show a restless baby squirming in her mother's lap, a toddler clumsily holding a shovel and a bucket, and a young girl sprawling in a large armchair. The emotional truth Cassatt arrested was heightened by her striking arrangements of keyed-up color and flat-tened space, over which brushstrokes seem to dance.

left: Mary Cassatt, *The Boating Party,* 1893/1894, oil on canvas, National Gallery of Art, Chester Dale Collection

above: Mary Cassatt, *Children Playing on the Beach,* 1884, oil on canvas, National Gallery of Art, Ailsa Mellon Bruce Collection

explore more

> "I have had a joy from which no one can rob me — I have been able to touch some people with my art."
> Mary Cassatt

A Girl and Her Puppy

Look closely at *Little Girl in a Blue Armchair*. What do you see?

Consider how the girl might feel. Which words might best describe her mood?

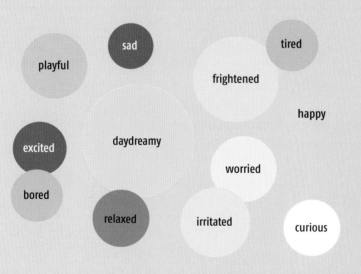

sad
playful
tired
frightened
happy
daydreamy
excited
worried
bored
relaxed
irritated
curious

Wonder: What might she be thinking about?

Imagine: If you could talk with this girl, what would you ask her? What might she ask you?

Pretend this painting is a scene from the middle of a story. Make up the rest of the story.

Who is the girl?

Where is she?

Why is she sitting in this chair?

What was she doing before this moment?

What will she do next?

How might the story end?

Create a series of drawings that tell a story about the girl and her dog.

Mary Cassatt, *Little Girl in a Blue Armchair*, 1878, oil on canvas, National Gallery of Art, Collection of Mr. and Mrs. Paul Mellon

1 Painting Life

American artist Winslow Homer (1836–1910) mastered both oil and watercolor painting during his career, portraying nineteenth-century America in a fresh way.

At age eighteen, Homer worked as an apprentice at a printing company in his hometown of Boston. He soon made a name for himself by drawing illustrations for novels, sheet music, magazines, and thirteen children's books.

He then moved to New York City, where he began painting and working as a freelance illustrator with the popular magazine *Harper's Weekly*. Homer received an assignment to report on the inauguration of President Abraham Lincoln, and he later covered the Civil War. His pictures of the Union troops received international acclaim.

In the late 1860s and 1870s, Homer turned his attention to rural life and scenes in coastal America, especially outdoor scenes of people at work and play: children exploring, farm girls attending to their duties, sportsmen hunting and fishing. After the destruction of the Civil War, these warm and appealing images perfectly suited the country's mood and hopes for a simpler, more innocent time.

2 Breezing Up

Sailing home after a day at sea, a fisherman and three boys return with their catch. The late afternoon sun casts a shadow on the sail, and rays of sunshine light the boys' shoulders and arms. In the distance gray clouds gather across the blue sky. A brisk breeze fills the sail and pushes the little boat along choppy waves. Everyone leans to one side to balance the boat as its sail catches the wind, and cool sea spray splashes on them as their boat cuts through the water. The boy holding the tiller looks off to the horizon.

top: Thomas Faris and Thomas A. Gray, *Winslow Homer*, 1863, albumen silver print, National Portrait Gallery, Smithsonian Institution, Washington. Photo credit: National Portrait Gallery, Smithsonian Institution / Art Resource, NY

middle: Winslow Homer, *On the Stile*, c. 1878, watercolor, gouache, and graphite on wove paper, National Gallery of Art, Collection of Mr. and Mrs. Paul Mellon

bottom: Winslow Homer, *On the Trail*, c. 1892, watercolor over graphite, National Gallery of Art, Gift of Ruth K. Henschel in memory of her husband, Charles R. Henschel

3 Masterful Watercolorist

Homer created his first series of watercolor paintings in Gloucester, Massachusetts, in 1873. By the time he painted his last watercolor in 1905, he had earned an international reputation as a watercolorist.

Homer traveled widely—to the Adirondacks, Virginia, Canada, Bermuda, Florida, the Caribbean, and throughout New England. During these working trips, he preferred to paint with watercolors because they were easy to carry, and he could work outdoors and observe nature directly. He used watercolors to record the activities and environment that were specific to each place. With quick brushstrokes, he captured crashing waves, moving animals, and the visual effects of changing light. To suggest sunlight, Homer left areas of the white paper untouched. Using this technique, the whiteness of the paper—and not the paint—creates glints of brilliant light.

Watercolor Sketch

You will need:
A set of watercolor paints
Watercolor brush
A pad of watercolor paper
Sponge
Cup of water

Homer liked to paint with watercolors because the medium allowed him to experiment freely. Since watercolors are easy to carry, he could go out into nature and make sketches on the spot. Watercolors can be used in various ways. Here's one technique to try when painting water and sky in landscapes.

Experiment with wet paper effects

• Wet a piece of paper with a sponge before you begin painting.

• Brush short, light strokes of color onto the wet paper, and watch the paint spread.

• Layer on other colors; let them run into each other.

• Use this technique to create a landscape— orange, yellow, and pink for a sunset sky; deep blue, green, and purple for an ocean; brown, red, and orange for a mountain range.

• Let the paint and paper dry before you add details, such as people, animals, trees, and buildings.

"You will see, in the future I will live by my watercolors." Winslow Homer

top: Winslow Homer, *Salt Kettle, Bermuda*, 1899, watercolor over graphite, National Gallery of Art, Gift of Ruth K. Henschel in memory of her husband, Charles R. Henschel

bottom: Winslow Homer, *Red Shirt, Homosassa, Florida*, 1904, watercolor over graphite, National Gallery of Art, Gift of Ruth K. Henschel in memory of her husband, Charles R. Henschel

2 Mouthwatering Memories

Thiebaud's paintings bring up memories of birthday parties, family picnics, and holidays at home. Perhaps they serve as a reminder of a favorite bakery or a special outing. Many of Thiebaud's works provide a glimpse of his own childhood memories, such as eating his mother's baked goods or selling hot dogs and ice cream cones on the boardwalk of Long Beach when he was a teenager. At their root, his paintings reflect his deep affection and nostalgia for the rituals and traditions of American life.

Cakes, a large canvas with thirteen colorfully frosted confections, is one of the most delectable examples of Thiebaud's work. These treats in a window display are instantly recognizable: Boston cream pie, chocolate layer cake, angel food cake, and strawberry birthday cake. Which cake would you like to taste?

1 A Hungry Artist

Wayne Thiebaud (born 1920) grew up during the Great Depression and has spent most of his life living and working in California. He tried cartooning and commercial art, but eventually his passion for painting and art history led him back to school to study art education and studio art. In 1951 Thiebaud began a dual career as an art teacher and an artist in Sacramento, California. Over the next ten years he experimented with compositions based on familiar subjects and his childhood memories, such as pinball machines and ice cream cones. By the 1960s Thiebaud's "delicious" still-life paintings of round cakes, slices of pie, colorful lollipops, hot dogs, cherries, cheese, chocolate truffles, and candy apples had made him a truly original American artist.

"You take a lemon meringue pie. It's quite a beautiful thing.... It's more than just a subject, it's also a kind of relationship to the paint itself. You really feel like you're sort of making the meringue and ... working with the pie."
Wayne Thiebaud

top left: Wayne Thiebaud (detail), 1975, (photo: Mimi Jacobs). Archives of American Art, Smithsonian Institution

bottom right: Wayne Thiebaud, *Candy Apples*, 1987, woodcut on Tosa Kozo paper, National Gallery of Art, Gift of Kathan Brown

far right: Wayne Thiebaud, *Cakes*, 1963, oil on canvas, National Gallery of Art, Gift in Honor of the 50th Anniversary of the National Gallery of Art from the Collectors Committee, the 50th Anniversary Gift Committee, and The Circle, with Additional Support from the Abrams Family in Memory of Harry N. Abrams

3 Like Frosting

Thiebaud's subjects might be light and fun, but his approach to painting is serious. He uses still-life subjects to explore formal qualities of painting: color, line, shape, light, composition, and texture. Like the cakes, his paintings are deliciously layered.

Texture: Thiebaud became famous for his ability to use paint in unexpected ways to recreate the look and feel of the substance it depicts. In *Cakes,* he painted each dessert with thick, heavy strokes to produce a textured surface. He transformed the oil paint into dense, buttery frosting or thick whipped cream. In other works, his paint "becomes" meringue, candy, or even mustard.

Line, shape, and composition: Like a baker arranging a window display, Thiebaud carefully composes his works. *Cakes* shows a repeating pattern of cylinders set against a blank background. The artist places the cylinder cakes on impossibly tall stands, which create perfect elliptical shadows. Each cake and its stand are outlined to reinforce the shapes.

Light and color: Thiebaud's colors are more complicated than they seem—the white frosting is not just white, but it is also orange, blue, and beige. The cakes cast bluish-purplish shadows. Thiebaud developed a practice of sketching with different colored paints, which produces the rainbowlike lines that define the edges of his objects.

try this

"[My subject matter] was a genuine sort of experience that came out of my life, particularly the American world in which I was privileged to be. It just seemed to be the most genuine thing which I had done." Wayne Thiebaud

To make the frosting, mix about five parts tile grout to one part paint. Stir in brown paint to make chocolate frosting, pink paint to make strawberry frosting, green paint for mint frosting, etc. The tile grout will air dry, so place it in a covered storage container to keep it soft.

To decorate the cake, use the palette knife to spread the frosting all over the surface of the box. Then use the decorating tips to create lines and shapes—perhaps a heart, flowers, or face—or to write words. Top the cake with plastic berries and decorations.

Think about: What occasion is your cake for? How do chefs express themselves artistically?

Set the cake aside. It will dry in a few hours, depending upon the thickness of the tile grout. Don't forget to put a label next to it: "Art. Do not eat!"

Sweet Sculpture

You will need:

For your cake: papier-mâché boxes (round, square, rectangular—the size of a cake, pie, or cupcake)

For the frosting: Elmer's tile grout (one quart covers about three cakes)

To color the frosting: Acrylic paint (brown, pink, yellow, green, violet)

To decorate the cake: Palette knives and a cake decorating set (pastry bags and tips)

To top the cake: plastic berries or flowers (optional)

Mixing spoon
Covered plastic containers
Apron

top left: Wayne Thiebaud, *Dark Cake,* 1983, woodcut on hand-made Tosa Kozo paper, National Gallery of Art, Gift of Kathan Brown

top right: Wayne Thiebaud, *Chocolates,* 1993, color hard-ground etching with drypoint on Somerset Satin white paper, National Gallery of Art, Gift of Kathan Brown

bottom: Wayne Thiebaud, *Meringue,* 1995, color aquatint with drypoint on Somerset White Textured paper, National Gallery of Art, Gift of David A. Blanton III

What subjects would reflect your daily life?

questioning traditions

Many artists experiment with materials and techniques to create new forms of art. Giuseppe Arcimboldo created imaginative "portraits" with the eye of a scientist in the sixteenth century. Johannes Vermeer studied light effects in timeless scenes set in seventeenth-century Holland, and Joseph Mallord William Turner pushed the painting of light and atmosphere to the edge of abstraction. A constant innovator, Pablo Picasso explored the expressive powers of color early in his career. The twentieth century was filled with artists questioning and expanding the definition of art, from the surrealist vision of Joan Miró to the cubist still lifes of Diego Rivera, collage techniques of Romare Bearden, drip and splatter process of Jackson Pollock, and comic book images of Roy Lichtenstein. As you look at the different works in this chapter, think about the many ways an artist might be an innovator.

> **"These pictures are all the more amazing as nobody had ever created anything similar."**
> **Gregorio Comanini, *Il Figino*, 1591**

1

Peculiar Portraits

Giuseppe Arcimboldo (1526–1593) was born into a family of painters in the northern Italian city of Milan. The city was considered the cradle of naturalism, a mode of artistic expression based on the direct observation of nature. This approach to art was shaped by Leonardo da Vinci, whose work Arcimboldo likely studied in Milan.

In 1563, at the age of thirty-six, Arcimboldo left Italy to work in the imperial courts of the Habsburg rulers, first for Maximilian II in Vienna and then for Rudolf II in Prague. He served as court painter for twenty-five years, creating portraits of the imperial family. Like other artists of his time, he designed tapestries and stained glass windows, and created theater costumes for the elaborate festivals and masquerades he organized at the court. However, Arcimboldo remains best known for the highly original "portraits" he composed by imaginatively arranging objects, plants, animals, and other elements of nature.

To celebrate the reign of Emperor Maximilian II, Arcimboldo presented two series of composite heads: *The Seasons* and *The Elements*. In *The Seasons* (*Spring, Summer, Autumn,* and *Winter*), created in 1563, Arcimboldo combined plants associated with a particular season to form a portrait of that time of year. The series was extremely popular in the Habsburg court, and Arcimboldo reproduced it several times so the emperor could send versions to friends and important political figures. Three years later he completed a series on the four elements (*Earth, Air, Fire,* and *Water*). Arcimboldo also made witty composite portraits of different professions, such as a librarian, jurist, cook, and vegetable gardener, using objects associated with each occupation. In these innovative works, Arcimboldo fills the paintings with dense details that come together harmoniously to create a human form.

2 When Art Meets Science

When Arcimboldo arrived at the court of Emperor Maximilian II, he found his new patron was passionately interested in the biological sciences of botany and zoology. The study of flora and fauna grew as a result of the voyages of exploration and discovery that were undertaken to the New World, Africa, and Asia in the sixteenth century. Explorers returned with exotic plants and animals that created an explosion of European interest in the study of nature. Maximilian transformed his court into a center of scientific study, bringing together scientists and philosophers from all over Europe. His botanical gardens and his zoological parks with elephants, lions, and tigers caused a sensation.

As court painter to the emperor, Arcimboldo had access to these vast collections of rare flora and fauna. His nature studies show his skill and precision as an illustrator and his knowledge as a naturalist—but Arcimboldo went beyond illustration by building fantastic faces out of the natural specimens he observed. His paintings not only demonstrate a unique fusion of art and science, but they also provide an encyclopedia of the plants and animals that Maximilian acquired for his botanical garden and menagerie.

Maximilian displayed Arcimboldo's paintings of the seasons and elements in his *Kunstkammer,* a special "art chamber" dedicated to his collections of marvelous and curious things. Along with works of art, he collected Greek and Roman antiquities, scientific instruments, precious gems, fossils, and interesting shells. Arcimboldo's paintings fit right in among the emperor's many prized possessions.

top left: Giuseppe Arcimboldo, *Water*, 1566, oil on limewood, © Kunsthistorisches Museum Vienna, Austria

From *The Elements* series, this painting combines more than sixty different fish and aquatic animals.

bottom left: Giuseppe Arcimboldo, *The Librarian*, 1562, oil on canvas, Skoklosters Castle (photo: Samuel Uhrdin)

In this portrait of the court historian Wolfgang Lazius, the artist used an open book for his full head of hair, feather dusters for his beard, keys for his eyes, and bookmarks for his fingers.

right: Giuseppe Arcimboldo, *Four Seasons in One Head,* c. 1590, oil on panel, National Gallery of Art, Paul Mellon Fund

3 Four Seasons in One

Look closely at *Four Seasons in One Head*. A gnarled and knotty tree trunk creates the figure's head and chest, representing the winter season. Two holes in the trunk form the eyes, a broken branch serves as a nose, and moss and twigs are the beard. Spring flowers decorate the figure's chest. Summer is indicated by the cherries that form the ear, the plums at the back of the head, and the cloak of straw draped around the shoulders. Apples, grapes, and ivy, the fruit and plants of autumn, top the head. On a branch among the apples, Arcimboldo inscribed his name in the wood beneath the bark that has been stripped away: "ARCIMBOLDUS F" (F is for *fecit,* which means "made this" in Latin).

This is one of the last paintings that Arcimboldo created after he returned to Milan from the Habsburg court in 1587. Perhaps he considered it a self-portrait in the "winter" of his life, brooding over his bygone seasons.

Imagine that this portrait could talk. What stories might it tell?

It's Seasonal!

Explore Arcimboldo's *The Seasons*. List at least five things the artist incorporated into the paintings to suggest each season. How does each painting remind you of a particular season?

Compare: How are the four paintings similar? How are they different?

Create a composite portrait of a season

You will need:
A cardboard, wood, or canvas surface
Clear-drying glue, such as PVA or Mod Podge
A brush
Collage materials — newspapers, magazines, decorative papers, stickers, etc.

Choose a season for the subject of your work. Collect collage materials that remind you of that season, such as twigs, leaves, and photographs of activities that you enjoy at that time of year.

Start by making an outline of a human profile on your board or canvas, indicating generally where the eyes, nose, ears, and mouth might be. This will serve as a guide as you arrange your collage materials.

Cut out and arrange parts for your collage. Experiment with overlapping pieces and turning them in various directions. Consider how different shapes can be combined to create a human head. Keep

in mind your color palette and how it can help communicate the mood or feel of the season. When arranging collage pieces, start with larger shapes to cover the area of the head, then use smaller pieces to create details and facial features.

Once you have arranged the collage elements, begin to glue them down. Brush glue on the underside to adhere to the board or canvas. When you are finished, brush a thin layer of glue on top of the entire work to prevent the edges from curling.

Try this again with a different subject. Consider choosing a profession, a school subject, or a holiday. You might even want to create a series, as Arcimboldo did.

top left: Giuseppe Arcimboldo, *Winter*, 1573, oil on canvas, Louvre, Paris, France (photo: Jean-Gilles Berizzi). Photo credit: Réunion Musées Nationaux / Art Resource, NY

top right: Giuseppe Arcimboldo, *Spring*, 1573, oil on canvas, Louvre, Paris, France (photo: Jean-Gilles Berizzi). Photo credit: Réunion Musées Nationaux / Art Resource, NY

bottom left: Giuseppe Arcimboldo, *Summer*, 1573, oil on canvas, Louvre, Paris, France (photo: Jean-Gilles Berizzi). Photo credit: Réunion Musées Nationaux / Art Resource, NY

bottom right: Giuseppe Arcimboldo, *Autumn*, 1573, oil on canvas, Louvre, Paris, France (photo: Gérard Blot). Photo credit: Réunion Musées Nationaux / Art Resource, NY

1

Painter of Light

Dutch artist Johannes Vermeer (1632–1675) is famous for his paintings of intimate, quiet scenes of everyday life in the seventeenth century. His paintings are especially treasured because they are so rare—only thirty-five of his paintings survive, and none of his personal writings or drawings has been found.

Much about Vermeer's life and career remain a mystery. He lived most of his life in Delft, a wealthy trading city in the Dutch Republic. His father was an innkeeper and art dealer, so Vermeer must have been surrounded by art as a child. It is not known where or with whom he trained, but his early work was as a history painter, specializing in scenes from ancient history, mythology, religion, and literature. Vermeer soon developed a special interest in genre scenes. In these images of daily life, he painted small-scale views of domestic scenes, such as musical concerts or women writing letters. Since these are not portraits of specific people, his paintings tend to have a timeless, universal quality.

After his death at the age of forty-three, Vermeer's reputation as an artist faded, probably because he left behind few works. After Vermeer's work was "rediscovered" in the nineteenth century, his masterful technique, delicate use of light and shadow, and poetic simplicity became greatly admired.

2

A Life in Balance

In *Woman Holding a Balance,* a woman stands quietly, looking down at a perfectly balanced scale. She wears an elegant blue jacket trimmed with white fur, and she stands in front of a table that holds coins, pearls, gold, and other precious objects. A large painting of a religious scene hangs on the wall behind her.

This painting presents themes and characteristics found in many paintings by Vermeer.

A moment in time: It captures a moment that seems to be frozen in time forever. His works leave us wondering: What might happen next?

Looking into a private world: This woman is lost in her own thoughts as she gazes at the balance held in her right hand. Vermeer presents a quiet, intimate scene of a solitary figure. His works make us curious: What might the woman be thinking or feeling? Why is she holding the balance?

Sunlight and shadows: Daylight streaming through the window on the left casts a diagonal beam of light across the scene. The woman's face and hands are illuminated, and the pearls and gold glimmer in the light. Meanwhile, the rest of the scene is dark with shadows, creating a sharp contrast.

A limited palette of colors: Vermeer created his tranquil paintings by using just a few tones and shades, including yellow, ochre, brown, gray, and ultramarine blue. These color tonalities give the painting a visual harmony.

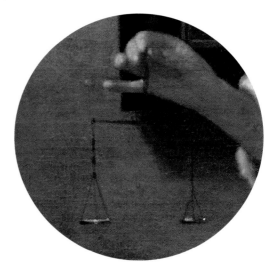

Contemplative Moments

Woman Holding a Balance shows a scene of everyday life, but it is also an allegory—it uses a story and characters to represent a larger idea about the moral and spiritual aspects of being human. Common in Dutch genre scenes of the seventeenth century, allegories reminded viewers not to let the wealth and prosperity of the times distract them from important spiritual goals.

Pearls, gold jewelry, and coins—references to earthly beauty and wealth—spill from a jewelry box and spread across the table in front of her. The large painting hanging behind her shows the Last Judgment, part of the end of the world as described in the Bible. Paintings of the Last Judgment remind viewers to consider their actions and decisions carefully because they will be assessed and weighed at the end of time. Vermeer added one more important object to the scene: a small framed mirror that hangs on the left wall directly opposite the woman's face. Artists often used mirrors to symbolize self-reflection or self-awareness.

Through this tranquil painting, Vermeer emphasizes that riches and wealth are not the most important things in life. Instead, people should lead a balanced, harmonious life, one spent in moderation and self-reflection, and weigh their worldly possessions with their spiritual life.

Both *A Lady Writing* and *Woman Holding a Balance* show moments of thoughtful attention. Consider other similarities as well as differences between the paintings.

The lady at her writing desk looks as if she has been interrupted. What might she be thinking? At whom might she be looking? To whom might she be writing?

Many of the same objects—pearl necklace and earrings, jewelry box, fur-trimmed coat, table draped with blue fabric, chair with lion head finials—appear in Vermeer's paintings. This leads art historians to believe that he had these props in his studio and reused them to compose different scenes.

far left: Johannes Vermeer, *Woman Holding a Balance*, c. 1664, oil on canvas, National Gallery of Art, Widener Collection

above: Johannes Vermeer, *A Lady Writing*, c. 1665, oil on canvas, National Gallery of Art, Gift of Harry Waldron Havemeyer and Horace Havemeyer, Jr., in memory of their father, Horace Havemeyer

explore more

Vermeer and the *Camera Obscura*

People have long wondered how Vermeer was able to create paintings that look like snapshots. Before photography was invented in the nineteenth century, it was unusual for paintings to have this quality. This has led some to believe that Vermeer may have studied light effects through a *camera obscura* (Latin for "dark room"). Used since the Renaissance, this pinhole device projects an image onto a wall surface with the aid of a lens. Scientists and mathematicians utilized it for astronomical observation, and some artists employed it to aid in topographical drawing. With the study of optics and the development of lenses (for microscopes and telescopes) in the Dutch Republic during the seventeenth century, the *camera obscura* became yet another way for artists and scientists to study the world during this time of great exploration and discovery.

Although he did not paint in a darkened room and copy images from a camera, Vermeer noted the particular effects of the *camera obscura* and adeptly translated them in his compositions. *Girl with the Red Hat* is a good example of some of the phenomena observed through a camera. The girl, wearing a large "Turkish" style hat and draped in blue fabric, is seated in a chair (with lion head finials similar to the one in *A Lady Writing*). She turns around as if she's been interrupted, her mouth open as if she is about to speak.

Effects of the *camera obscura*:

A focused and unfocused (blurry) areas

B composition: figures and objects are cropped at the edge of the picture, which occurs when you look at a scene through a lens and box

C flattened space (shallow depth of field): it's hard to tell that a tapestry is on the wall behind her, and you don't feel a great sense of space in the room

D sharp contrasts of light and shadow

E intensification of color

F diffused highlights (halation): this occurs when light hits a reflective surface. Vermeer often painted these areas with dabs of white to exaggerate their effect; up close they look abstract.

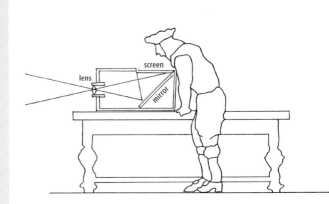

above: Johannes Vermeer, *Girl with the Red Hat*, c. 1665/1666, oil on panel, National Gallery of Art, Andrew W. Mellon Collection

The diagram to the left shows a simple *camera obscura*: a box with a lens, mirror, and glass screen. Light travels through the lens, reflects off the surface of the mirror, and projects an image from the world onto the glass.

1 A British Master

During his long career, Joseph Mallord William Turner (1775–1851) painted a wide range of subjects: seascapes, topographical views, historical events, mythology, modern life, and imaginary scenes. Turner's innovative focus on light and the changing effects of atmosphere made his landscapes enormously popular and influential.

Born in London, Turner was the son of a barber who sold the boy's drawings by displaying them in the window of his shop. Turner decided to become an artist at the age of fourteen, and he enrolled in the school of the Royal Academy of Art, the leading art society in Great Britain. Ambitious as well as talented, he was elected the youngest member of the Royal Academy eight years later, at the age of twenty-two. In 1807 he was appointed professor of perspective at the Royal Academy, a position he held for thirty years. His father assisted him in the studio for many years.

Although he lived in London all his life, Turner traveled extensively across Britain and throughout Europe. By closely observing nature and sketching outdoors, he recorded his visual experience of landscapes and his emotional responses to them. His sketchbooks served as a type of memory bank for ideas he used months and even years later. Three hundred of Turner's sketchbooks still exist.

Joseph Mallord William Turner, *Self-Portrait* (detail), c. 1799, Tate, Bequeathed by the Artist, 1856. © Tate, London 2007. Photo credit: Tate, London / Art Resource, NY

2 An Illuminating Scene

Turner visited Tyneside, a town near Newcastle in northeast England, in 1818, but he did not paint *Keelmen Heaving in Coals by Moonlight* until 1835, almost twenty years later. This scene shows a view of Tyneside's busy harbor. Coal was the essential source of power at the time of the Industrial Revolution in the nineteenth century, and the Newcastle region was the mining and industrial center of Britain.

The shallow Tyne River flows through rich coal fields, and flat-bottomed barges, called keels, transported the coal. Keelmen ferried coal from mines up the river to the mouth of the harbor, where they shoveled the coal into specially designed ships known as colliers. These boats were loaded at night so they could sail with the morning tide down the coast to London. Turner depicts keelmen transferring coal in the glow of moonlight and torchlight.

Although Turner's painting describes a scene of contemporary trade and industry, light is the true subject of his composition. Light from the full moon illuminates the cloudy sky and glitters on the calm water. Dark boats and silhouetted figures frame the view and draw attention across the distance and out to sea. Capturing the drama of a night sky over water, Turner makes nature a central focus of this work.

3 Painterly Technique

To convey mood and atmosphere, Turner also experimented with painting techniques. In a rather unconventional way, he applied paint with a palette knife, a tool usually reserved for mixing colors.

Turner painted some areas of *Keelmen Heaving in Coals by Moonlight* more thickly than others, such as the silvery white moon and the yellow-orange torchlights. In this technique of applying paint thickly to a canvas, called impasto, the artwork often retains the mark of the brush or palette knife. Turner's heavy application and thick paint create a textured surface that allows the raised areas on the canvas to catch light.

Joseph Mallord William Turner, *Keelmen Heaving in Coals by Moonlight*, 1835, oil on canvas, National Gallery of Art, Widener Collection

try this

Atmospheric Effects

Turner traveled abroad several times, touring Belgium, the Netherlands, Denmark, France, Austria, Germany, Switzerland, and Italy. He filled his sketchbooks on these summertime trips, and he returned home to work on oil paintings during the winter. In his luminous landscapes that combine memory and imagination, Turner describes weather conditions as if he had made his oil paintings on the spot.

Turner's imagination was most captivated by the Italian city of Venice. Its location on the water provided numerous opportunities for the artist to explore light and color. The two paintings here, made nearly a decade apart, illustrate the development of Turner's artistic style.

The earlier work, *Venice: The Dogana and San Giorgio Maggiore,* shows the bustling activity along and in the Grand Canal, as gondolas transport goods and people. Turner features two important sites: the church of San Giorgio Maggiore and the Dogana, or Customs House. The water sparkles with radiant sunlight and reflects the buildings and boats.

In *The Dogana and Santa Maria della Salute, Venice,* Turner's later style is a study of atmospheric effects. Details of architecture, boats, and people are minimized, and the light seems to evaporate the solid forms of the buildings and boats. Few of Turner's contemporaries understood his later works with their poetic haziness, but these paintings greatly influenced future generations of artists.

top: Joseph Mallord William Turner, *Venice: The Dogana and San Giorgio Maggiore*, 1834, oil on canvas, National Gallery of Art, Widener Collection

At the "especial suggestion" of a British textile manufacturer, Turner devised this Venetian cityscape as a symbolic salute to commerce. Gondolas carry cargoes of fine fabrics and exotic spices. On the right is the Dogana, or Customs House, topped by a statue of Fortune. *Keelmen* was painted as a companion piece to this picture. When displayed together, the two paintings present a comparison between great maritime and commercial powers, Venice and Great Britain.

bottom: Joseph Mallord William Turner, *The Dogana and Santa Maria della Salute, Venice*, 1843, oil on canvas, National Gallery of Art, Given in memory of Governor Alvan T. Fuller by The Fuller Foundation, Inc.

Paint with a palette knife

Challenge yourself to create a landscape or cityscape scene using only a palette knife, a traditional tool usually used for mixing paint. Experiment with it, and find out how many different ways you can use it.

You will need:
**Thick acrylic paint or tempera thickened
   with wallpaper paste
Mounted canvas, foamboard, or
   white cardboard
A metal or plastic palette knife**

Experiment

• Squeeze or spoon one color of paint onto your painting surface. Use the palette knife to spread the paint and create a design.

• Think about how you use the palette knife to move the paint. Spread the paint thin (like buttering toast), then make swirls of thicker paint (like frosting a cupcake). How will you cover areas of the surface to indicate sky, land, and sea?

• Use the tip or edge of the palette knife to scratch lines into layers of paint, that is, draw by removing paint. Use this process to add buildings, trees, people, and other details to your landscape.

• Gradually add one or two more colors, mixing them with the palette knife.

Reflect: How did this technique feel? What were its challenges? What effects did you create that you wouldn't have been able to do with another tool?

"A painter paints to unload himself of feelings and visions." Pablo Picasso

1 Early Years in Paris

Pablo Ruiz Picasso (1881–1973) was one of the most inventive artists of all time. He continually searched for fresh ways to represent the world, and he is admired for his experimentation with different styles, materials, and techniques. The years 1901 to 1906 are often described as Picasso's Blue and Rose periods because he was exploring the way color and line could express his ideas and emotions.

Born in southern Spain, Picasso studied at art academies in Barcelona and Madrid. He first visited Paris, then the center of the art world, in 1900 at the age of nineteen, and he was captivated by the vibrant city and its museums and art galleries. Four years later Picasso settled in Paris, and France became his adopted home.

2 Why So Blue?

Being an immigrant to Paris, Picasso sympathized with the city's poor and hungry people, with their struggles and their sense of isolation. He also felt great sorrow over the death of his best friend. These feelings literally colored his works. From 1901 to 1904 Picasso experimented with using dark, thick outlines to create figures and shapes on his canvas. He filled in the outlines with lighter and darker tones of blue. *The Tragedy*, one painting from his Blue period, shows three unnaturally tall, thin figures on an empty beach.

Consider: How might the people be feeling?

left: Pablo Picasso at Montmartre (detail), Place Ravignan, c. 1904, Musée Picasso, Paris. Réunion Musées Nationaux / Art Resource, NY (photo: RMN-J. Faujour)

above: Pablo Picasso, *The Tragedy*, 1903, oil on wood, National Gallery of Art, Chester Dale Collection © 2013 Estate of Pablo Picasso / Artists Rights Society (ARS), New York

Feeling Rosy

"Colors, like features, follow the changes of the emotions." Pablo Picasso

A few years later, Picasso began to paint with lighter and more delicate colors, such as rosy pinks, reds, and warm browns. He also discovered a new subject of interest: the circus. He was fascinated by the clowns and acrobats who performed in the Cirque Médrano, which was based in Montmartre (his neighborhood in Paris). Picasso felt a strong connection with these *saltimbanques,* or street performers. They were all outsiders who worked here and there, making art. The entertainers who appear in his paintings and drawings, however, are not shown performing. Instead, Picasso presents them in quiet, unexpected moments. These years, from late 1904 to early 1906, are called Picasso's Rose or circus period.

Family of Saltimbanques shows a circus family in a sparse setting. A harlequin, or jester, wears a diamond-patterned suit. He holds the hand of a young girl in a pink dress carrying a basket of flowers. A large clown in a red costume and two young acrobats—one holds a tumbling barrel—complete the circle. A woman with a hat decorated with flowers sits off to one side.

Wonder: What is the relationship among the people?

Compare: How are these two paintings similar? How are they different? Which words best describe each painting?

cold

delicate

sad

warm

bleak

strong

mysterious

frail

silent

somber

dreamy

isolated

Pablo Picasso, *Family of Saltimbanques*, 1905, oil on canvas, National Gallery of Art, Chester Dale Collection © 2013 Estate of Pablo Picasso / Artists Rights Society (ARS), New York

Watercolor Resist Painting

To better understand how artists communicate feelings, experiment with color and contour line to create a "moody" watercolor resist painting.

You will need:
Crayons
Watercolor paints and brush
Watercolor paper

In the works from his Blue and Rose periods, Picasso explored line and color. He used dark, heavy outlines—called contour lines—to define the figures and shapes in his paintings. He then limited his palette to only a few colors so he could focus on the emotional quality of the scene.

Ask your family or friends to strike a pose for you. Take some time to study the poses. Try tracing the outlines of the figures in the air with your finger. On a piece of watercolor paper, use a pencil to draw the contour lines of the figures and objects you see. Trace over your lines with a crayon. Press hard to make the lines thick.

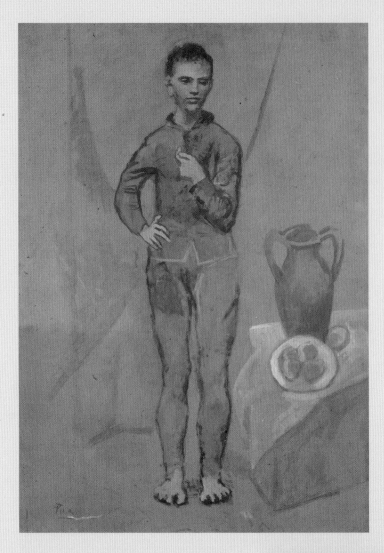

top: Pablo Picasso, *Juggler with Still Life*, 1905, gouache on cardboard, National Gallery of Art, Chester Dale Collection © 2013 Estate of Pablo Picasso / Artists Rights Society (ARS), New York

bottom: Pablo Picasso, *Le Gourmet*, 1901, oil on canvas, National Gallery of Art, Chester Dale Collection © 2013 Estate of Pablo Picasso / Artists Rights Society (ARS), New York

Next, decide which mood or emotion you wish to communicate in your painting. Choose two colors that might best express that feeling. Use this limited watercolor palette to paint over the crayon lines. Cover the entire paper with color. Create light and dark shades by adding more or less water to the paint. Mix the two colors together to create a third color.

Discover: The lines made with the wax crayon will show through, or resist, the watercolor. This results in a painting made of both lines and colors.

1 Catalan Painter

Joan Miró (1893–1983) was born, educated, and trained as an artist in Barcelona, Spain. Although the art scene in Barcelona was lively, Miró moved to Paris in 1920, seeking a more cosmopolitan environment. There he met a fellow Spanish artist, Pablo Picasso. Miró was inspired by the interlocking shapes and facets of Picasso's cubist art. Another influence on Miró's style was his contact with the many other avant-garde artists—particularly Dada and surrealist poets—who lived and worked in Paris.

At the same time, Miró remained deeply attached to Catalonia, the northeast corner of Spain where he grew up. Each summer he returned to his family's farm in Montroig, a village near Barcelona. Parts of the landscape of Catalonia—plants, insects, birds, stars, sunshine, the moon, the Mediterranean Sea, architecture, and the countryside—appear in Miró's art throughout his long career. He began *The Farm* in Montroig in the summer of 1921. The artist continued to work on it in Barcelona, and he completed it nine months later in his studio in Paris.

American writer Ernest Hemingway—Miró's friend and occasional sparring partner at a boxing gym in Paris—purchased *The Farm* as a birthday present for his first wife, Hadley, in 1925 or 1926. The painting later hung in Hemingway's homes in Key West, Florida, and Havana, Cuba. The author once wrote, "Miró was the only painter who had been able to combine in one picture all that you felt about Spain when you were there and all that you felt when you were away and could not go there."

2 The Farm

This painting is a "portrait" of a cherished place, an inventory of Miró's life on his farm in Catalonia.

Look closely to find:

A large eucalyptus tree (its dark leaves are silhouetted against the brilliant blue sky)

Footsteps along a path

A barking dog

A woman washing clothes at a trough, with her baby playing nearby

A donkey plodding around a millstone

Mountains

Families of rabbits and chickens in a coop

A pig peeking through an open door

A goat with a pigeon perched on its back

A lizard and snail crawling amid grass and twigs

Buckets, pails, and watering cans littering the yard

A farmhouse with a horse resting inside and a covered wagon propped outside

Wonder

What time of day is it? Is that the sun or a full moon in the sky?

Whose footprints are those? Why do they suddenly end?

What might be making the dog bark?

above: Joan Miró in his Barcelona studio (detail), 1914, (photo: Francesc Serra), Arxiu Històric de la Ciutat de Barcelona – Arxiu Fotogràfic

right: Joan Miró, *The Farm*, 1921–1922, oil on canvas, National Gallery of Art, Gift of Mary Hemingway

"This picture represents all that was closest to me at home, even the footprints on the path by the house.... I am very much attached to the landscape of my country. That picture made it live for me." Joan Miró

3 How Surreal!

Although Miró never officially joined the surrealist group, André Breton, its founder, remarked, "Miró is the most surrealist of us all." Surrealist artists tried to release the creative power of the subconscious mind by making images in which the familiar meets the fantastic. Miró wanted to depict the things he envisioned in his mind as well as those he saw with his eyes. This way, he could demonstrate the power of imagination to transform reality.

The Farm is an example of how Miró made the ordinary extraordinary. The scene is both real and unreal. It feels familiar, yet unfamiliar. Daily events in the farmyard are meticulously rendered, each element carefully observed and precisely described, yet the overall effect is strangely dreamlike. Miró's style—fanciful and playful, while wonderfully detailed and thoughtfully arranged—creates a kind of magical realism.

Touch Drawing Exercise

José Pascó was Miró's teacher at the Barcelona School of Fine Arts. He encouraged his young pupil to experiment. Years later, in 1948, Miró recalled, "Pascó was the other teacher whose influence I still feel.... Color was easy for me. But with form I had great difficulty. Pascó taught me to draw from the sense of touch by giving me objects which I was not allowed to look at, but which I was afterwards made to draw. Even today... the effect of this touch drawing experience returns in my interest in sculpture: the need to mold with my hands, to pick up a ball of wet clay like a child and squeeze it. From this I get a physical satisfaction that I cannot get from drawing or painting." Pascó tried to stimulate Miró's senses and make him become more aware of his surroundings. He wanted his student not only to rely on what he saw but also to work from what he felt and imagined.

Experiment: Make a drawing of something that you cannot see!

You will need:
Two large paper bags (a grocery bag will do)
Paper
Colored pencils, crayons, or markers

This activity requires two people. Each of you should secretly choose a safe object— a stuffed animal, toy, flower, hairbrush, spoon, keys, an item of clothing—and place it in a paper bag so the other person cannot see it. (Don't choose a dangerous object with sharp edges.)

Feel: Take turns reaching into each other's bag and touching the mystery object inside. Use your hands and your imagination, but not your eyes. Feel the entire object from front to back, top to bottom, and side to side. Think about the object's size and shape. Describe its textures. Is it smooth, bumpy, soft, rough, hard, or a combination of textures? Does it remind you of anything?

Imagine: Close your eyes, keeping your hand on the mysterious object in the bag. Imagine that this object is a new species. Where might it live? What might it eat? What sounds would it make? Does it fly, swim, crawl, or run? Imagine that the object came from another planet. What could it be? Imagine that the object is a building. What is its purpose? What or who is inside? What is the environment like around it? Imagine that the object is a kind of food. How would it taste?

Next, without looking in the bag, make a drawing inspired by the object. Describe the object's shape and texture as well as ideas that formed in your imagination. Draw without stopping to worry about the final result. Surprise yourself!

Reflect: How did this experience help you think about the object differently?

top: Joan Miró, *Shooting Star*, 1938, oil on canvas, National Gallery of Art, Gift of Joseph H. Hazen. Copyright © 1998 Board of Trustees, National Gallery of Art, Washington

bottom: Joan Miró, *Figure and Birds*, 1948, color lithograph, Paris 1974, no. 231, National Gallery of Art, Gift of Mr. and Mrs. Burton Tremaine

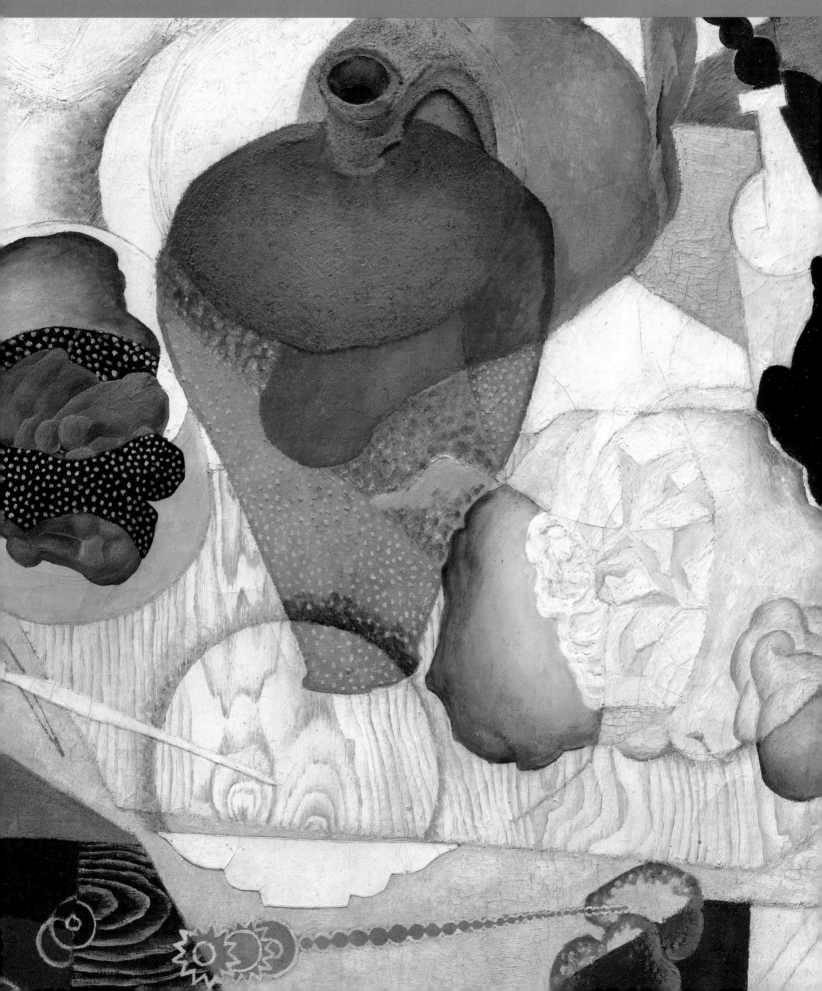

1 Mexico's Modernist

Diego María Rivera (1886–1957) was born in the small town of Guanajuato in central Mexico. He moved with his family to Mexico City in the early 1890s. Both of his parents were school teachers. As a way to encourage his son's artistic talent, Rivera's father covered the walls of the boy's room with canvas so that he could draw on them. By the age of twelve, Rivera had already finished high school, and he entered San Carlos Academy, the national art school of Mexico. Rivera studied works by Mexican painters, collected Mexican folk art, and traveled great distances to see the art of Mexico's ancient Maya and Aztec cultures. In this way he gained a deep respect for his country's traditions.

From 1910 to 1920, a decade marked by the Mexican Revolution and World War I, Rivera resided in Europe on a grant of money from the government of Mexico. By the age of twenty-one he had lived and worked in Spain, Italy, and France. He was inspired by Spanish art, wall frescoes from the Italian Renaissance, and the bold new style of modernism. In Paris, Rivera met many artists, including Pablo Picasso and Georges Braque. They were developing a new artistic style called cubism, which was a daring way of visualizing three-dimensional objects on a flat surface, such as paper or canvas. Picasso and Braque challenged themselves to show several views or sides of an object simultaneously. This cubist technique makes objects in their works look broken up and then reassembled.

Diego Rivera, *Self-Portrait* (detail), 1941, Smith College Museum of Art, Northampton, MA. Gift of Irene Rich Clifford

2 Spanish Still Life

In his own experimentation with cubism, Rivera painted *No. 9, Nature Morte Espagnole* (Spanish Still Life) in boldly simplified shapes. Look for circles, triangles, and rectangles. Which objects do you recognize? Overlapping rectangles show a table viewed both from above and the side. Where did Rivera paint patterns to imitate the wood grain of the table top?

A large earthenware jug at the center of the table casts a blue-green shadow. Surrounding it are glass bottles, fruits, and vegetables, all shown from multiple views. On the left, Rivera included a *molinillo,* a small wooden whisk used to mix the ancient Mexican drink *chocolate de agua.* For hundreds of years, Mexicans have used *molinillos* to whip hot chocolate into a frothy drink. When making his cubist paintings in Europe, Rivera often included things that reminded him of Mexico. Can you find all three views of the *molinillo*?

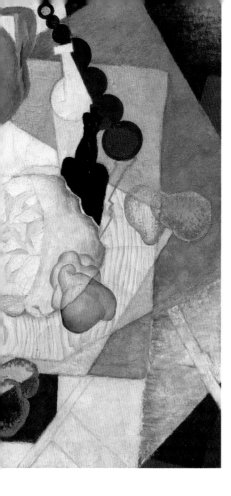

left: Diego Rivera, *No. 9, Nature Morte Espagnole*, 1915, oil on canvas, National Gallery of Art, Gift of Katharine Graham

below: Molinillo (photo: Donna Mann, National Gallery of Art)

4 Celebrating Mexican Culture

When he returned to Mexico, Rivera combined the painting techniques he had learned in Europe with his passion for his homeland. He focused on the history and daily life of ordinary Mexicans, particularly factory workers, farmers, and children. In the 1920s and 1930s Rivera became famous for the large murals he painted on the walls of public buildings. He believed art should be seen and enjoyed by all people. Through his murals he told powerful stories about the struggles of the poor, and he emphasized the history and diverse peoples of Mexico. When he died in 1957, Rivera was honored for creating a modern Mexican art that celebrated his country's native traditions.

3 Rivera's Technique

Rivera varied colors and textures to make his paintings more visually interesting. His cubist compositions are distinctive for their bright colors. To add texture, he applied paint thickly in some places or covered areas with little dabs. Sometimes he mixed sand or sawdust into his oil paint to give it a rough texture. Rivera used a variety of textures in *No. 9, Nature Morte Espagnole*. The paint is so thick at the mouth of the jug that it resembles real clay. It almost seems water could be poured through the opening!

"My cubist paintings are my most Mexican."
Diego Rivera

Diego Rivera, *Friday of Sorrows on the Canal at Santa Anita*, from *A Vision of the Mexican People*, 1923–1924, mural. Secretaria de Educacion Publica, Mexico City © 2013 Banco de México Diego Rivera and Frida Kahlo Museums Trust/Artist Rights Society (ARS), New York. Photo credit: Schalkwijk/Art Resource, NY

This mural is part of a cycle showing the history of the Mexican people from the time of the great Aztec civilization.

Cubist Still Life

Diego Rivera's *No. 9, Nature Morte Espagnole* is an example of his early experimentation with cubism. Flowers, fruit, books, musical instruments, bottles, bowls, or other objects are carefully arranged in still-life paintings. Some artists paint these objects so convincingly that they fool your eye into thinking they're real. Other painters, such as the cubists, make it difficult to identify the items.

Cubism was pioneered in the early 1900s by Pablo Picasso and Georges Braque, who were influenced by Paul Cézanne's use of multiple viewpoints in a single painting. The way cubists represented the world was considered to be radical: they fractured form, shifted viewpoints, confused perspective, and flattened volume. Their work often resembled a collage and sometimes even included collage elements, like newspaper. They wanted to show several different views of one thing in a picture—the front, the back, inside, and outside all at the same time.

A Cubist Approach to Drawing

You will need:
Paper
Paints, colored pencils, or markers

First, gather ordinary objects from your home or, like Rivera, include things that have a special meaning to you. Make the composition interesting by selecting objects with distinct colors, patterns, shapes, and textures. Arrange the objects on a table in a way that pleases you.

Next, draw what you see in your still life arrangement. Focus on basic shapes— spheres, cubes, and cylinders—and textures.

Then, draw your still life from a different viewpoint. Draw some objects while standing up, draw a few from another side, and draw some by looking up at them from below.

Reflect: What are the challenges of drawing three-dimensional objects on a flat piece of paper?

from top to bottom:

Paul Cézanne, *Still Life with Apples and Peaches*, c. 1905, oil on canvas, National Gallery of Art, Gift of Eugene and Agnes E. Meyer

Juan Gris, *Fantômas*, 1915, oil on canvas, National Gallery of Art, Chester Dale Fund

Pablo Picasso, *Still Life*, 1918, oil on canvas, National Gallery of Art, Chester Dale Collection © 2012 Estate of Pablo Picasso / Artists Rights Society (ARS), New York

Georges Braque, *Still Life: Le Jour*, 1929, oil on canvas, National Gallery of Art, Chester Dale Collection

1 Bearden's Journey

Born in Mecklenburg County in North Carolina, Romare Bearden (1911–1988) was just three years old when his family moved from the rural South to a vibrant section of New York City called Harlem, a growing center of African American life and culture. There, Bearden grew up amid the city's diverse people, the new sounds of jazz, and a wide variety of art, including paintings by Pablo Picasso and sculpture from Africa. When he decided to become an artist, Bearden had the knowledge and experiences of Harlem from which to create his art. He also drew from his memories of his return trips to North Carolina to visit his grandparents and of the summers he spent working in steel mills in Pittsburgh when he was a teenager.

3 Piece by Piece

To make this image, Bearden began by collecting patterned papers, including magazine illustrations, wallpaper, and hand-painted papers. He cut them into shapes and glued them onto a large piece of canvas, layering the pieces to make the picture. Bearden described his technique as "collage painting" because he often painted on top of the collaged papers.

Look closely

Can you find paper that was cut and repeated throughout the collage? Bearden used the same hand-painted blue paper for the woman's dress, the man's clothing, and the water barrel at his feet.

How were the faces made? Bearden arranged as many as fifteen different magazine cuttings for the man's face, hands, and eyes. He was particularly interested in hands and eyes because they help express a person's character and thoughts.

Do you see the train rolling across the horizon? Trains appear in many of Bearden's collages. They reminded the artist of his travels between the North and the South when he was a child. In African American history, trains sometimes symbolize the Underground Railroad, the escape from slavery, and the Great Migration to jobs in the North and West after Emancipation.

2 An Artist's Memories

Tomorrow I May Be Far Away melds Bearden's memories of the people, landscape, and daily activities of Southern communities. In the center, a man is seated in front of a cabin. A woman peers through the cabin window, her hand resting on the sill. Behind them is a lush landscape filled with birds, a woman harvesting a melon, and another cabin.

Imagine: What are the man and woman watching? What might happen next? Create a story to go along with this scene.

"Aah, tomorrow I may be far away
Oh, tomorrow I may be far away
Don't try to jive me, sweet talk can't make me stay"
From "Good Chib Blues," first recorded in 1929

try this

Bearden's Photomontages

A photomontage is a collage that includes photographs. In *Watching the Good Trains Go By*, Bearden used photographs to create a rural scene that reminded him of Mecklenburg County in North Carolina. Cut-out pictures of trains, faces, and arms, combined with patterned papers, create a busy scene.

Bearden's art was influenced by his love for jazz and the blues. Music was often the subject of his work, and it also influenced his way of working. One distinguishing feature of jazz is improvisation. In this approach, performers create music in response to their inner feelings and the stimulus of the immediate environment. Bearden advised a younger artist to "become a blues singer—only you sing on the canvas. You *improvise*—you find the rhythm and catch it good, and structure as you go along—then the song is you."

"The more I played around with visual notions as if I were improvising like a jazz musician, the more I realized what I wanted to do as a painter, and how I wanted to do it."
Romare Bearden

Create a photomontage

You will need:
Scissors
A glue stick
Cardboard or tag board
Assorted papers, wallpaper sample books, magazines, and/or postcards
Personal photographs

First, think of a place that is special to you. Like Bearden, use your memories of everyday life in that place to inspire your work. What sights and sounds, people, and activities make that place special?

Next, gather photographs and postcards that remind you of that place. Collect patterned papers, such as wrapping paper or wallpaper, and look through magazines for images that remind you of your special place. Cut out patterns and images from your papers, and then arrange and glue them on the cardboard to form the background.

Then, cut out details of people and objects from your photographs. Overlap and layer the pieces to create your scene.

Improvise as you go!

top: Romare Bearden, *Watching the Good Trains Go By*, 1964, collage of various papers on cardboard, Columbus Museum of Art, Ohio: Museum Purchase, Derby Fund, from the Philip J. and Suzanne Schiller Collection of American Social Commentary Art 1930–1970. Art © Romare Bearden Foundation / Licensed by VAGA, New York, NY

bottom: Bearden working in his Long Island City Studio (detail), early 1980s, Estate of Romare Bearden, courtesy of the Romare Bearden Foundation (photo: Frank Stewart)

Jackson Pollock

A New Process

In 1945 Pollock and his wife, artist Lee Krasner, moved to the east end of Long Island. Working in an unheated barn beside his farmhouse, he combined his earlier creative experiments to produce an entirely new way to paint. Dipping sticks or hardened brushes into cans of house paint, Pollock poured, flung, and dripped paint onto large canvases spread on the barn's floor. (He used commercial house paint because it is thinner and flows more freely than traditional artist's paints.) Pollock relied on his intuition and his body to infuse his images

"My painting does not come from the easel.... On the floor I am more at ease. I feel nearer, more a part of the painting, since this way I can walk around it, work from the four sides and literally be *in* the painting." **Jackson Pollock**

Action Painter

Born in Cody, Wyoming, Jackson Pollock (1912–1956) became one of the most original American artists of the twentieth century. He was the youngest of five brothers. His mother encouraged all of her sons to become artists, and three of them did. While he was growing up, Pollock's family moved around the American West, but when he was eighteen years old, Pollock moved to New York City to become an artist.

Pollock discovered a wide range of styles and art forms that influenced his artistic development: the expressive style of contemporary Mexican muralists, the dream images of surrealists, the lyrical lines of Asian calligraphy, the raw force of works by Pablo Picasso, and the physical process involved in creating Navajo sand paintings. Pollock felt driven to express his emotions through painting.

with emotional force. His process was not all physical, however, for Pollock spent a lot of time thinking about the canvas at his feet before setting his paint in motion. By carefully controlling his movements, he directed gentle spatters, thin arcs, and powerful diagonals of color onto his canvas. The "drip paintings" Pollock made from 1947 to 1951 were unlike any paintings people had seen before that time. They caused a sensation and established a new way of making art—one that made the act of creation visible.

3 Lavender Mist

More than seven feet in height and nearly ten feet wide, *Number 1, 1950 (Lavender Mist)* is one of Pollock's most recognized paintings.

Imagine you could step inside this painting

What would it feel like?

Which line or arc would you like to follow? Where would it take you?

How would you move in, around, and under the colors?

Pollock made dense, intricate layers with white, blue, yellow, silver, umber, rosy pink, and black paint. He didn't use any lavender paint on the canvas, but where the pink and the blue-black colors meet, it looks like lavender. When Pollock's friend, art critic Clement Greenberg, saw the painting, he said it felt like "lavender mist." This atmospheric description became the painting's subtitle.

Pollock's handprints are visible at the upper left and right edges of the canvas. These are literal traces of the artist's presence *in* the work.

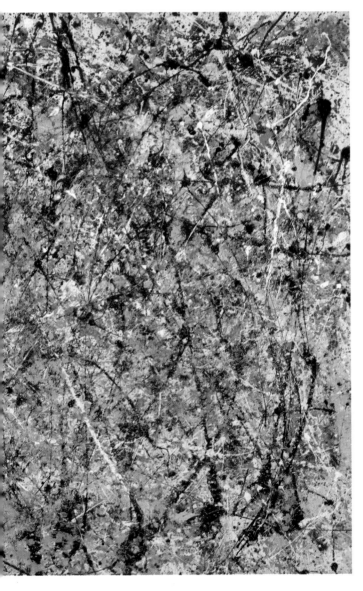

top and right: Photographs of Jackson Pollock painting *Autumn Rhythm: Number 30, 1950* by Hans Namuth, silver gelatin prints, © Estate of Hans Namuth, courtesy Pollock-Krasner House and Study Center, East Hampton, NY

left: Jackson Pollock, *Number 1, 1950 (Lavender Mist)*, 1950, oil, enamel, and aluminum on canvas, National Gallery of Art, Ailsa Mellon Bruce Fund

Paint Without Brushes!

Jackson Pollock's revolutionary art bypassed traditional ways of painting. He invented a method that was uniquely his own. Now it's your turn to experience the action of making a painting without using a paintbrush. This activity requires special materials and can be a bit messy. Get permission from your parents or other adults first!

You will need:
Newspaper (to cover your work area)
Smock or big, old shirt (to protect your clothes)
Large sheet of white paper or butcher paper
Washable tempera paints
Paper cups or bowls (for the paint)
Look around for materials to paint with:
   old mittens
   popsicle sticks
   cotton swabs
   string
   straws
   sponges
   combs
   forks
   spoons
   paper tubes
   spatulas

Process

After covering the floor of the work area with layers of newspaper, place a sheet of white paper in the center of the space. Give yourself enough room to walk around all sides of it. You might enjoy listening to music while you work. (Jackson Pollock liked to listen to jazz.)

Work with one color at a time. Dip a popsicle stick or another item into one container of paint. Experiment with different methods of painting.

swirl
splash
pour
squirt
overlap
squiggle
drip
fling
smudge
splatter
dribble

Move your whole body—not just your arm and hand—to reach all areas of the paper. Fill the paper from edge to edge to create an allover pattern.

Experiment with different types of lines: thick, thin, short, long, straight, curved, parallel, diagonal. Vary the height, angle, and speed of your actions.

Think about how to layer your colors. Pause and wait until one color is dry before adding a layer of a different color.

Remember there are no mistakes. Chance occurrences are part of making art!

Jackson Pollock, *Untitled*,
1951, ink on Japanese paper,
O'Connor/Thaw 1978, no. 812,
National Gallery of Art, Gift
of Ruth Cole Kainen

"When I am painting I have a general notion as to what I am about. I can control the flow of the paint.... There is no accident, just as there is no beginning and no end."
Jackson Pollock

"This was the first time I decided to make a painting really look like commercial art. The approach turned out to be so interesting that eventually it became impossible to do any other kind of painting." Roy Lichtenstein

Lichtenstein kept this painting, one with personal significance, in his possession until he and his wife gave it to the National Gallery in 1990.

1 Pop!

In the 1950s and 1960s, young British and American artists made popular culture their subject matter. By incorporating logos, brand names, television and cartoon characters, and other consumer products into their work, these artists blurred the boundaries between art and everyday life.

Roy Lichtenstein was one of the originators of this new pop movement. Fascinated by printed mass media, particularly newspaper advertising and cartoon or comic book illustration, Lichtenstein developed a style characterized by bold lines, bright colors, dot patterns, and sometimes words.

"The art of today is all around us."
Roy Lichtenstein

2 Roy

Born and raised in New York City, Roy Lichtenstein (1923–1997) began to draw and paint when he was a teenager. During this time he also developed a passion for jazz and science, and he enjoyed visiting museums. He went to Ohio State University to study fine arts, but his college years were interrupted when he was drafted into the army and sent to Europe during World War II. After returning to Ohio State and completing his studies, Lichtenstein worked as a graphic designer and taught art at several universities. In the 1960s he quickly emerged as a leading practitioner of pop art. This success allowed him to dedicate himself full-time to making art.

3 A Big One

Lichtenstein's breakthrough came in 1961 when he painted *Look Mickey*. It is one of his earliest paintings to use the visual language of comic strips. The idea for the painting came from a scene in the 1960 children's book *Donald Duck: Lost and Found,* a copy of which probably belonged to the artist's sons.

Lichtenstein used the design conventions of the comic strip: its speech bubble, flat primary colors, and ink-dot patterns that mimic commercial printing. These Benday dots became Lichtenstein's trademark. Invented by Benjamin Day in 1879, the dots were used in comic strips and newspapers as an inexpensive way to print shades and color tints. Look at Donald's eyes and Mickey's face: Lichtenstein made those dots by dipping a dog-grooming brush into paint and then pressing it on the canvas! He later used stencils to help him paint dots.

"It's a matter of re-seeing it in your own way."
Roy Lichtenstein

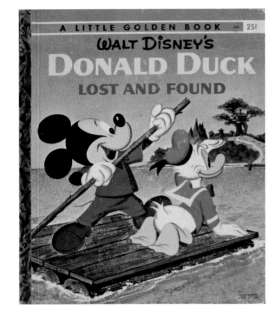

First they went fishing at Catfish Cove.
"Look, Mickey," cried Donald. "I've hooked a big one."
"Land it," laughed Mickey, "and you can have it fried for lunch."

Cover and illustration by Bob Grant and Bob Totten from Carl Buettner, *Donald Duck: Lost and Found,* 1960. © 1960 Disney

4 Look!

Lichtenstein often enlarged, simplified, and reworked images he found. He never copied the source.

Compare the storybook illustration with Lichtenstein's painting. What parts are similar? What differences can you find?

Examine the changes the artist made

He simplified the background by removing three people

He rotated the direction of the dock

He added the word bubble, which makes the text a part of the picture

He translated the illustration into an image in primary colors, using red, blue, and yellow on a white background

By making paintings that look like enlarged comic strips, Lichtenstein surprised and shocked many viewers. Why? He made people think about where images come from and how they are made.

Moving Toward Abstraction

In his *Bull* series of 1973, Lichtenstein explored the progression of an image from representation to abstraction. Beginning with a recognizable drawing of a bull, Lichtenstein simplified, exaggerated, and rearranged the colors, lines, and/or shapes until the animal was almost unrecognizable. This series reveals the "steps" of the artistic process: the body of the bull is reduced to geometric shapes of triangles and squares, the blue areas refer to the bull's hide, and curved lines suggest the horns and tail.

Study the images

How are the pictures similar? How are they different?

Which one do you find most intriguing? Why?

Would you know the last one is a picture of a bull if you didn't see it in this series?

Create a series of your own

Start with a photograph of a place, person, or object. You can take the photo yourself, or cut one out of a magazine or newspaper.

Then, create a series of two, three, or more drawings. Make each one more abstract by simplifying the shapes, colors, and lines. Reduce them each time until you can no longer recognize your subject.

Bull I, no. 116

Bull II, no. 117

Bull III, no. 118

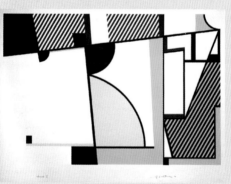

Bull IV, no. 119

Bull V, no. 120

Bull VI, no. 121

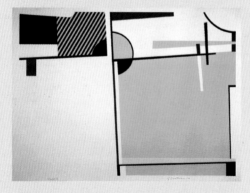

Roy Lichtenstein, 1973, National Gallery of Art, Gift of Gemini G.E.L. and the Artist

How might you
experiment as an artist?

playing with space

From representation to abstraction, sculpture takes art off the wall. All the artists introduced in this chapter thought innovatively in three dimensions. Edgar Degas modeled wax sculptures as a way to better understand form and motion. Interested in a different kind of movement, Alexander Calder constructed mobiles that activate space. Dan Flavin used fluorescent lights to create bright sculptures that shape and color the surrounding space. Martin Puryear crafts ambiguous forms that invite wonder. As you compare the artists in this chapter, think about the characteristics that are unique to sculpture.

Edgar Degas, *Four Dancers*,
c. 1899, oil on canvas, National
Gallery of Art, Chester Dale
Collection

Edgar Degas, *Self-Portrait
(Edgar Degas, par lui-même)*
(detail), probably 1857, etching,
National Gallery of Art, Rosenwald Collection

1 The Artist at the Ballet

Edgar Degas (1834–1917) lived in Paris, the capital and
largest city in France, during an exciting period in the
nineteenth century. In this vibrant center of art, music,
and theater, Degas attended ballet performances as often
as he could. At the Paris Opéra, he watched both grand
productions on stage and small ballet classes in rehearsal
studios. He filled numerous notebooks with sketches
to help him remember details. Later, he referred to his
sketches to compose paintings and model sculpture he
made in his studio. His penetrating observations of ballet
are apparent in his numerous variations on the subject.

2 Off Stage

Degas made more than a thousand drawings, paintings,
and sculptures on ballet themes. Most of his works
do not show the dancers performing onstage. Instead,
they are absorbed in their daily routine of rehearsing,
stretching, and resting. Degas admired the ballerinas'
work — how they practiced the same moves over and
over again to perfect them — and likened it to his
approach as an artist.

Four Dancers depicts a moment backstage, just before
the curtain rises and a ballet performance begins. The
dancers' red-orange costumes stand out against the
green scenery. Short, quick strokes of yellow and white
paint on their arms and tutus catch light and, along
with squiggly black lines around the bodices, convey
the dancers' excitement as they await their cues to
go onstage.

Here's a mystery. Did Degas depict four different dancers,
or is this four views of one dancer? It could be just one
ballerina, pivoting in space, shown in the progression of
the motion.

3 A Dancer's Life

Dance students at the Paris Opéra often came from working-class families. It was an exhausting life: members of the ballet corps rehearsed all day and hoped to dance onstage in the evening. Few of them became star ballerinas.

Marie van Goethem, a student who lived near Degas, posed for *Little Dancer Aged Fourteen*. The daughter of a tailor and a laundress, she had two sisters who also studied ballet and modeled for Degas. Three years after this sculpture was made, Marie was dismissed from the Opéra because of her low attendance at ballet classes. It is not known what happened to her.

Degas's sculpture also had trouble. Standing almost life-size, it is made of clay and wax. Degas tinted the wax in fleshlike tones and dressed the figure in a ballet costume, with tiny slippers and a wig tied low with a silk ribbon. People were both fascinated and repelled by how lifelike it looked, and they debated whether it was art. Some viewers thought the sculpture was so realistic it belonged in a science museum alongside specimens! After Degas died in 1917, copies of this wax figure were cast in plaster and bronze, and *Little Dancer Aged Fourteen* grew in fame around the world.

Try to imitate Marie's pose. The slight sway in her lower back, arms clasped behind her, chin upraised, eyes closed, and legs turned out indicate she is in the casual fourth position, a stance that ballet dancers assume when they are at rest. Instead of depicting the dancer in movement, this sculpture focuses on a psychological state.

"I think with my hands." **Edgar Degas**

4 Working from the Inside Out

Degas worked on *Little Dancer Aged Fourteen* for more than two years. X-radiographs of the sculpture reveal what is inside. The artist began with a metal armature, which serves as a sort of skeletal support. He used wood and material padding to make the thighs, waist, and chest thicker. Next, he wrapped wire and rope around the head, chest, and thighs. To create the arms, he used wire to attach two long paintbrushes to the shoulders. Degas modeled the figure first with clay to define the muscles, and then he modeled the final layer of the sculpture in wax.

Degas had satin slippers, a linen bodice, and a muslin tutu made for the figure. A wig of human hair, braided and tied with a ribbon, completed the illusion. A coat of wax, spread smoothly with a spatula over the surface of the sculpture, gives it an overall waxy look.

Edgar Degas, *Little Dancer Aged Fourteen*, 1878 – 1881, yellow wax, hair, ribbon, linen bodice, satin shoes, muslin tutu, wood base, National Gallery of Art, Collection of Mr. and Mrs. Paul Mellon

explore more

Balancing Act

Degas was a prolific artist, making more than a thousand paintings. He was admired for his drawing skills, particularly his work in pastels, and he was known for his experimentation with printmaking and photography. Degas's sculpture is a puzzling aspect of his career. His largest figure, *Little Dancer Aged Fourteen,* is the only one he ever publicly exhibited, even though he made hundreds of wax statuettes over four decades. These works, which were discovered in the artist's studio after his death, were posthumously cast in bronze. The National Gallery owns more than fifty of these wax sculptures.

The smaller wax statuettes, such as those shown here, were part of Degas's working process. They essentially serve as three-dimensional sketches that probably helped the artist better understand proportion, poses, balance, and movement of form in space.

Try to imitate the pose

An arabesque is a ballet position in which a dancer balances on one leg while extending the other leg back. At the same time, the dancer stretches his or her arms to the side as a way to provide balance. It's hard to hold this position for a long time! That's because it is part of a continual movement, and Degas is showing just one "paused" moment in time.

Ballet requires focused control and balance, and Degas had to think carefully about weight and balance when he made sculptures. He began by creating an armature,

a framework inside and sometimes outside a work to hold the position. He twisted and bent the wire into the pose he desired. Degas preferred to sculpt with wax that he often combined with a non-drying clay called plastilene. He could easily model and rework the statuettes as much as he wanted, making adjustments to the position. With the armature providing support, Degas was free to experiment with ways to convey the lightness, energy, and motion of a dancer. An active movement, such as the arabesque, makes the space around the sculpture dynamic.

An x-radiograph reveals the metal armature inside the sculpture.

top: X-radiograph image of *Arabesque over the Right Leg, Right Hand near the Ground, Left Arm Outstretched (First Arabesque Penchée),* X-ray and photograph, Conservation Laboratory, National Gallery of Art

middle: Edgar Degas, *Arabesque over the Right Leg, Right Hand near the Ground, Left Arm Outstretched (First Arabesque Penchée),* c. 1885/1890, brown wax, National Gallery of Art, Collection of Mr. and Mrs. Paul Mellon

bottom: Edgar Degas, *Arabesque over the Right Leg, Left Arm in Front,* c. 1885/1890, yellow-brown wax, metal frame, National Gallery of Art, Collection of Mr. and Mrs. Paul Mellon

1 A Playful Engineer

Alexander Calder (1898–1976) was born into a family of artists in Lawnton, Pennsylvania. Known as Sandy to friends and family, Calder loved to tinker. When he was eight years old, his parents gave him tools and a workspace where he constructed toys and gadgets with bits of wire, cloth, and string. He earned a college degree in mechanical engineering, but unsatisfied with that line of work, he enrolled in art school in New York City and became a newspaper illustrator.

Moving to Paris in 1926 proved to be a pivotal moment in his life. Calder made imaginative, miniature circus animals and performers similar to the toys he invented as a child. He then created a whole circus, complete with balancing acrobats and a roaring lion, and he put on performances for his friends. These circus characters, assembled of wire, cork, cloth, and string, were an early form of moving sculpture. Through the popularity of "Calder's Circus," he met other artists living in Paris, including surrealist Joan Miró and Piet Mondrian, whose abstract paintings inspired him: "When I looked at [these] paintings, I felt the urge to make living paintings, shapes in motion." Calder then created his first motorized abstract sculptures, dubbed "mobiles" by his artist-friend Marcel Duchamp. Developing an ingenious system of weights and counterbalances, Calder eventually invented works that, when suspended, move freely with air currents. The mobiles combine Calder's sense of play with his interest in space, chance and surprise, movement, toys, and engineering.

Calder returned to the United States in 1933. He set up a studio in Connecticut, where he continued to produce innovative sculptures on both large and small scales. During his lifetime, he received more than 250 commissions from public and private institutions, including the National Gallery of Art.

"When everything goes right, a mobile is a piece of poetry that dances with the joy of life and surprise." **Alexander Calder**

above: Alexander Calder holding his mobile on a Parisian street, 1954 / Agnès Varda. Alexander Calder papers, 1926–1967. Archives of American Art, Smithsonian Institution

right: Alexander Calder, *Untitled*, 1976, aluminum and steel, National Gallery of Art, Gift of the Collectors Committee

previous page: Alexander Calder in his studio, c. 1950 / unidentified photographer. Alexander Calder papers, 1926–1967. Archives of American Art, Smithsonian Institution

2 A Monumental Challenge

In 1973, when the East Building of the National Gallery was under construction, Calder was asked to create a giant mobile to hang in the atrium space. After consulting with architect I. M. Pei, Calder made a maquette (a small three-dimensional model) for museum approval. The mobile's colorful organic shapes complemented Pei's geometric architecture.

After the design was approved, Calder faced the challenge of how to construct a mobile that was thirty-two times bigger than the size of its model. If it were constructed from steel, as he had originally planned, the finished work would weigh about 6,600 pounds. It would be so heavy that a motor would be required to make it move. Calder collaborated with artist-engineer Paul Matisse, who used unique aerospace technology to solve the weight and movement problems. Matisse fabricated the mobile's panels of high-strength honeycombed aluminum with thin skins. Although the panels appear to be solid steel, they are actually hollow and buoyant. In spite of its grand scale, the mobile weighs merely 920 pounds, moves solely on air currents, and maintains a sense of lightness and delicacy.

When asked to title the mobile, Calder replied, "You don't name a baby until it is born." The East Building mobile remains untitled because Calder died before it was hoisted up to the frame of the roof. Calder never saw the completion of his last, and one of his largest, mobiles. What would you name it?

3 Perfectly Balanced

Connected to the ceiling at only one point, the mobile has twelve arms and thirteen shaped panels that are clustered into two groups. The upper group, described as "wings," includes six black panels and one blue panel, all hanging horizontally. In contrast, the lower group consists of six vertical red panels, or "blades." To make it move on the air currents in the museum, these blades are fastened to the arms at an angle. The speed and direction of the mobile vary when the air hits it, just as the wind moves a boat when it fills a sail.

The mobile has an orbit of just over eighty-five feet. That's the average length of a blue whale! Calder carefully planned the arms to be different heights so the shapes will never collide. At times, the red blades brush close to the building's walls, but they playfully avoid contact by a few inches and then continue onward in slow revolution. Always changing, the graceful mobile inspires imagination. What does the mobile remind you of?

"I want to make things that are fun to look at."
Alexander Calder

"It wasn't the daringness of the performance nor the tricks or the gimmicks: it was the fantastic balance in motion that the performers exhibited."
Alexander Calder

above: Alexander Calder, *The Circus*, 1932, pen and black ink on wove paper, National Gallery of Art, Gift of Mr. and Mrs. Klaus G. Perls © 2000 Estate of Alexander Calder / Artists Rights Society (ARS), New York

right: Alexander Calder, *Rearing Stallion*, c. 1928, wire and painted wood, National Gallery of Art, Gift of Mr. and Mrs. Klaus G. Perls © 2000 Estate of Alexander Calder / Artists Rights Society (ARS), New York

"I think best in wire." Alexander Calder

Drawing with Wire

While a student at the Art Students League in New York City, Calder developed a talent for continuous line drawing, that is, creating an image with one single, unbroken line. He became a skilled draftsman while he worked for several newspapers in the city. Calder took his exploration of line into three dimensions when he began to create sculptures made of wire, a material he had loved since childhood.

Experiment with line in both two and three dimensions

You will need:
Paper
A pencil or pen
A single length of lightweight wire, such as plastic-coated electrical wire, copper, or brass wire from a hardware store

Choose a subject you can observe closely, such as a family member or friend, a flower, an object in your home, or an animal. Before you pick up your pencil, let your eyes wander over the edges of your subject.

Next, use your index finger to trace the outlines of the subject in the air, then try tracing them on your paper with your finger.

Finally, take your pencil and begin to draw. Work slowly without lifting the pencil until the figure is finished. Let the continuous line cross over itself and loop from one area to another. Continuous line drawings take practice, so try different ways to make several drawings of the same subject.

Now try it in wire! Think of wire as a single continuous line. Carefully bend and twist a piece of thin wire to create a three-dimensional "drawing" of your subject. To display your sculpture, stick the ends of the wire into a lump of clay or use string to suspend it.

Throughout his life, Calder experimented with materials and learned from them.

Reflect: What was challenging about making a continuous line drawing? What was different about making the sculpture? What did you learn from trying both?

1 Electric Light Art

American artist Dan Flavin had a bright idea: to make art with fluorescent lights!

Born and raised in Queens, New York, Dan Flavin (1933–1996) doodled and drew his way through school. He became an artist by taking art classes, reading a lot, and getting to know artists while he worked as a guard and elevator operator at museums in New York City. He made his first notes about "electric light art" while employed at the American Museum of Natural History. Flavin was soon constructing the works that would later make him famous.

2 Why Light? Why Not?

Traditional materials, such as paint, pastels, marble, or bronze, did not interest Flavin. Along with other artists of his generation, Flavin preferred to create art with ready-made materials that he could buy at the hardware store. First, he worked with light bulbs. Next, he experimented with fluorescent lights, and restricted his palette to ten colors: blue, green, pink, red, yellow, ultraviolet, and four kinds of white. The tubes were made in standard straight lengths of two, four, six, and eight feet, plus one circular shape. Flavin managed to make many variations with these limited colors and sizes.

"One might not think of light as a matter of fact, but I do. And it is . . . as plain and open and direct an art as you will ever find." Dan Flavin

above: Dan Flavin, *a primary picture*, 1964, red, yellow, and blue fluorescent light, Hermes Trust, U.K., Courtesy of Francesco Pellizzi (photo: Billy Jim), Courtesy Dia Art Foundation © Stephen Flavin / Artists Rights Society (ARS), New York

right: Dan Flavin installing *flourescent light, etc. from dan falvin,* at the National Gallery of Canada, Ottawa, 1969. Photo courtesy of Stephen Flavin © 2013 Stephen Flavin / Artists Rights Society (ARS), New York; courtesy of David Zwirner, New York / London.

Flavin dedicated this work to his friend and mentor, abstract artist Barnett Newman. He dedicated much of his work to friends, his beloved golden retriever Airily, and earlier artists he admired, such as Henri Matisse, Piet Mondrian, and Vladimir Tatlin.

3 It's Situational!

Flavin liked to create his art for unlikely locations—in corners, on the floor, between walls, across rooms, and around windows and doors.

Created for the corner of a room, *untitled (to Barnett Newman to commemorate his simple problem, red, yellow, and blue)* is made of six fixtures, each eight feet in length, with lamps facing different directions. Two yellow lights turn outward and form intense horizontal lines of color. Vertical blue and red lights are directed away from the viewer, creating a soft glow of color around the lights' metal pans. The corner of the room seems to disappear due to the reflected light and shadows on the walls, ceiling, and floor.

For Flavin, light was like paint. In his work, the colors of light blend in the air. As a result, the light transforms the surrounding space and architecture. That's why Flavin called his art "situational."

4 On and Off Art

What happens if a work stops working? The thought of burnt-out bulbs did not bother Flavin. He didn't consider his work to be permanent. Flavin made diagrams of his light sculptures to serve as certificates of ownership and to document the sizes, types, and colors of his light fixtures. At the National Gallery, the museum staff turns off the lights at night to conserve the bulbs.

fluorescent
poles
shimmer
shiver
flick

out

dim

monuments

of
on
and
off

art

try this

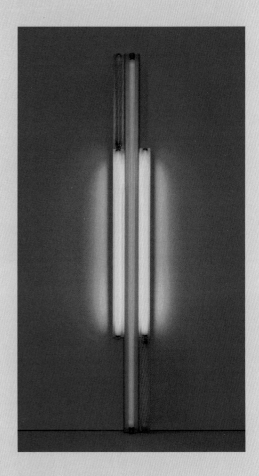

Light Poetry

Flavin wrote the poem above in 1961. Does it look like his art? You can almost imagine it as a vibrant pole of light. It's an example of a concrete poem, one that assumes the shape of its subject. A concrete poem about Halloween might be written in the shape of a pumpkin, or a poem about love could be written in the shape of a heart.

Poem by Dan Flavin, *untitled*, 10-2-1961

top right: Dan Flavin, *untitled (to Piet Mondrian)*, 1985, red, yellow, and blue fluorescent light, Collection Stephen Flavin (photo: Billy Jim), Courtesy Dia Art Foundation © Stephen Flavin /Artists Rights Society (ARS), New York

left: Dan Flavin, *"monument" for V. Tatlin*, 1969-1970, cool white fluorescent light, National Gallery of Art, Gift of the Collectors Committee

Create a poem about a work of art

Start by writing down words that come to mind when you look at the work. They can be descriptive, such as the colors of light and the shapes you see, or they can express your feelings about the art. Include verbs, adverbs, nouns, and adjectives in your list. Use these words to get you started:

dark radiant glow lines glare edge warm reflect mysterious brilliant space cool shining soft

Next, organize the words into phrases. Finally, arrange the phrases on a sheet of paper to form the shape of the work of art you selected.

Ron Bailey, *Martin Puryear in his studio, Chicago* (detail), 1987

1 A Craftsman at Heart

Abstract sculptures by Martin Puryear (born 1941) intrigue and surprise viewers with their puzzling shapes and forms. Born in Washington, DC, Puryear regularly visited the National Gallery of Art and the Smithsonian's Museum of Natural History as a child. These early experiences fostered his fascination with art, organic materials, and nature. The son of a postal worker who was a self-taught woodworker, Puryear began experimenting with wood as a teenager. He studied painting and printmaking in college and art school, but when he returned to the United States after living abroad for four years, he turned his attention to sculpture. Influenced by the many months he spent traveling the world, Puryear incorporates into his art the craft traditions of many cultures, including West African carving, Scandinavian design, boat building, basket weaving, and furniture making.

previous page: Martin Puryear, *Jackpot*, 1995, canvas, pine, and hemp rope over rubber, steel mesh, and steel rod, National Gallery of Art, Gift of Edward R. Broida

2 Working with Wood

An expert woodworker, Puryear makes his sculptures by hand with natural materials. Many of his sculptures show how they were constructed. Often the organic forms of his sculpture cannot be identified as specific objects, but they do suggest the shapes of animals, plants, or tools. This makes Puryear's sculptures appear both familiar and mysterious.

3 Lever No. 3

Lever No. 3 is a large sculpture with a heavy, massive body curving into a long, graceful neck that ends with a delicate circle. Puryear named this sculpture after the lever, a simple machine used to lift or move a heavy object by applying pressure at one point. Instead of looking like a tool, however, the sculpture resembles natural and biological forms. It might remind you of a plant tendril or an animal with a long neck.

Although at first glance it appears to be made of metal or stone, *Lever No. 3* is sculpted entirely of wood—Puryear's favorite material—by using traditional woodworking and boat-building techniques. To make this work of art, he bent thin planks of ponderosa pine into rounded shapes and then joined them together to create an even surface. The base, or body, of the sculpture looks heavy and solid, but it is actually a hollow, thin shell. After assembling the sculpture, Puryear coated it all over with black paint. The dark color hides the seams where the wooden planks are joined, but the artist sanded away the black paint in some areas to show the pattern of the underlying wood grain.

Consider: How might this sculpture look different if it were painted another color? How would it be different if it were made from another material, such as steel or feathers?

above: Martin Puryear, *Lever No. 3*, 1989, carved and painted wood, National Gallery of Art, Gift of the Collectors Committee

right: Martin Puryear, *The Charm of Subsistence*, 1989, rattan and gumwood, Saint Louis Art Museum. Funds given by the Shoenberg Foundation, Inc.

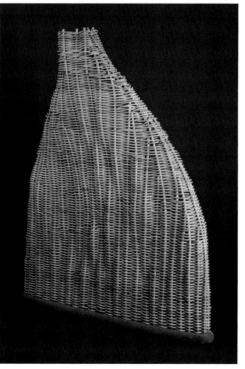

Build a Wood Sculpture

You will need:
**Spools, popsicle sticks, blocks, and
  scrap pieces of wood
Sandpaper
Wood glue**

First, sand any rough edges so the wood is smooth and free of splinters. Then, experiment with arranging the pieces into an interesting composition. Be inspired by the design of something in the world, or create a sculpture from your imagination. When building a sculpture, an artist has to consider height, width, and depth, and how the work looks from many points of view. Weight and balance are important to make the work stable.

Make a sketch of your design or take some notes to remember how all the pieces connect. Then, glue the pieces to each other one at a time, waiting a little bit for the glue to dry.

Lastly, give your work an interesting title.

top: Martin Puryear, *Old Mole*, 1985, red cedar, Philadelphia Museum of Art. Purchased with gifts (by exchange) of Samuel S. White III and Vera White and Mr. and Mrs. Charles C. G. Chaplin, and with funds contributed by Marion Boulton Stroud, Mr. and Mrs. Robert Kardon, Gisela and Dennis Alter, and Mrs. H. Gates Lloyd.

bottom: Martin Puryear, *Thicket*, 1990, basswood and cypress, Seattle Art Museum. Gift of Agnes Gund © Martin Puryear

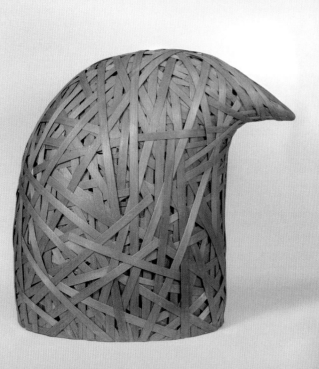

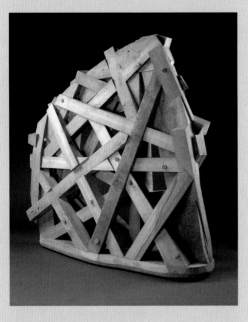

"I value the referential quality of art, the fact that a work can allude to things or states of being without in any way representing them."
Martin Puryear

What are different ways you might create a sculpture?

Timeline of Artists

- Italian
- Netherlandish
- Flemish
- Dutch
- French
- American
- British
- Spanish
- Mexican

Giotto, c. 1266–1337 / **72**

Fra Angelico, c. 1395–1455 / **69**

Rogier van der Weyden, c. 1399/1400–1464 / **73**

Fra Filippo Lippi, c. 1406–1469 / **69**

Leonardo da Vinci, 1452–1519 / **51**

Raphael, 1483–1520 / **73**

Giuseppe Arcimboldo, 1526–1593 / **121**

Peter Paul Rubens, 1577–1640 / **77**

Osias Beert the Elder, c. 1580–1624 / **99**

Hendrick Avercamp, 1585–1634 / **98**

Willem Claesz Heda, 1593/1594–1680 / **99**

Rembrandt van Rijn, 1606–1669 / **25**

Jan Davidsz de Heem, 1606–1683/1684 / **102**

Jan Steen, 1625/1626–1679 / **95**

Johannes Vermeer, 1632–1675 / **125**

Giovanni Paolo Panini, 1691–1765 / **32**

Canaletto, 1697–1768 / **29**

Claude-Joseph Vernet, 1714–1789 / **84**

John Singleton Copley, 1738–1815 / **81**

Jacques-Louis David, 1748–1825 / **58**

Élisabeth-Louise Vigée Le Brun, 1755–1842 / **55**

Joseph Mallord William Turner, 1775–1851 / **129**

John Constable, 1776–1837 / **3**

John James Audubon, 1785–1851 / **10**

George Catlin, 1796–1872 / **40**

Martin Johnson Heade, 1819–1904 / **7**

Jasper Francis Cropsey, 1823–1900 / **33**

Édouard Manet, 1832–1883 / **103**

Edgar Degas, 1834–1917 / **159**

Winslow Homer, 1836–1910 / **111**

Thomas Moran, 1837–1926 / **37**

Claude Monet, 1840–1926 / **11**

Mary Cassatt, 1844–1926 / **107**

Paul Gauguin, 1848–1903 / **59**

Augustus Saint-Gaudens, 1848–1907 / **85**

Vincent van Gogh, 1853–1890 / **59**

Henri Matisse, 1869–1954 / **41**

André Derain, 1880–1954 / **41**

Pablo Picasso, 1881–1973 / **133**

George Bellows, 1882–1925 / **45**

Diego Rivera, 1886–1957 / **141**

Georgia O'Keeffe, 1887–1986 / **15**

Joan Miró, 1893–1983 / **137**

Alexander Calder, 1898–1976 / **163**

Romare Bearden, 1911–1988 / **145**

Jackson Pollock, 1912–1956 / **149**

Jacob Lawrence, 1917–2000 / **89**

Wayne Thiebaud, born 1920 / **115**

Roy Lichtenstein, 1923–1997 / **153**

Dan Flavin, 1933–1996 / **167**

Chuck Close, born 1940 / **63**

Martin Puryear, born 1941 / **171**

Andy Goldsworthy, born 1956 / **19**

Acknowledgments

An Eye for Art was written by Nathalie Ryan with Molly Dalessandro and Heidi Hinish, with significant contributions from Sarah Stewart and Emily Hagan Lazaro. Staff members across the division of education likewise contributed to this project. In particular we wish to thank the many members and interns in the department of teacher, school, and family programs who assisted with the research and production of the *NGAkids Quarterly* over a decade and who drafted a new context for this publication: Anna Alexander, Nicole Anselona, Lorena Baines, Elizabeth Diament, Kim Hodges, Anastasia Karpova, Paula Lynn, Gina O'Connell, Emily Pegues, Zev Slurzberg, Katrine Solli, Elizabeth Tunick, Brandy Vause, and Jason Vrooman. We are grateful to the staff of the Gallery's publishing office, led by Judy Metro and Chris Vogel, including the book's designers, Wendy Schleicher and Rio DeNaro; editor Nancy Eickel and assistant editor Lisa Wainwright; photo coordinator Sara Sanders-Buell; production assistant Mariah Shay; as well as Amanda Sparrow, Julie Warnement, and Caroline Weaver for their earlier work on the *NGAkids Quarterly*. We also thank members of the department of imaging services for their essential support: Peter Dueker, Lorene Emerson, Barbara Wood, Ira Bartfield, and Kate Mayo. Finally, we thank the curators who reviewed the texts—Nancy Anderson, David Brown, Deborah Chotner, Harry Cooper, John Hand, Kimberly Jones, and Arthur Wheelock—and the entire National Gallery of Art curatorial staff, whose scholarly research was the source from which this book's content was drawn.